9x 9/11

Sci ✓

The World's
MOST BEAUTIFUL
Dolls

The World's MOST BEAUTIFUL *Dolls*

*Joan Muyskens Pursley
and Karen Bischoff*

KONECKY&KONECKY

Konecky & Konecky
156 Fifth Avenue
New York, N.Y. 10010

ISBN: 1-56852-032-8

Printed in Singapore

CONTENTS

INTRODUCTION

A doll is commonly defined as a small-scale figure of a human used as a child's plaything. We can never know where or when the first such figure was created specifically for play, since carved figures of the human form date back to prehistoric times. Archaeologists believe that the earliest figures had significance in the religious lives of the people who made and possessed them, and a scarcity of male figures predating 1000 B.C. suggests that they may have been fertility symbols. But that these figures were used only in religious rites is arguable, and there are doll experts who aver that the early human representations must have appealed to the children of those times just as today's dolls attract our children and serve as their companions for endless hours of imaginative play.

There is historical proof that young girls played with dolls during Ancient Greek and Roman times, and prints and paintings dating from the Middle Ages and the Renaissance show children holding or playing with dolls. Unfortunately, few dolls made prior to the 1700s exist today, so much of our knowledge of early dolls has had to be gleaned from literature and art. By the eighteenth century, beautiful and elaborately dressed dolls were being made in England, France, and Germany. The dolls most associated with that century are the woodens, as they have best withstood the passage of time. But many other materials were used for dolls in the 1700s, including china, papier-mâché, plaster, and wax.

What is known as the Golden Age of dollmaking, when china and bisque dolls were being mass-produced in France and Germany, dates from 1875 to 1930. During this period there was fierce competition between the French companies, such as Jumeau and Bru Jne. & Cie., and the German dollmakers, including Armand Marseille, Kämmer & Reinhardt, J. D. Kestner, Jr., and Simon & Halbig. These companies exported their dolls throughout Europe as well as to North America and Australia. The best examples dating from the Golden Age are truly lovely, having expressive faces and well-constructed bodies with jointed limbs. They must have been prized possessions of the children who owned them, just as they are of so many adult collectors today.

Although by definition dolls are playthings, throughout their history one finds doll-like figures designed for adults. Among them are the fashion figures that were used as mannequins for the display of contemporary clothing before the publication of fashion magazines; the eighteenth- and nineteenth-century automatons (animated figures), that were made primarily for the amusement of adults; and the twentieth-century boudoir dolls. Also called French cloth dolls, flappers, and bed dolls, the boudoir dolls originated in France about 1915 and had side-glancing eyes and overly long limbs. Most of them depicted young women dressed in the fashions of the times (pantsuits, dresses with shockingly short skirts, cloche hats, and high-heeled shoes) and one found them propped on beds and chairs in young women's abodes, or carried in the arms of flappers at speakeasies and Prohibition parties. During their heyday they were made by many companies—not just in France, but in Italy, England, and the United States—and of a variety of materials. Perhaps the first "art" dolls, they were sold in shops catering to adults and used as decorative accessories in and out of the home.

The boudoir doll faded from the American scene during the Depression, but a new kind of art doll has since taken its place. They are the limited-edition and one-of-a-kind dolls designed by artists specially for adult collectors. We call these objects "dolls" for lack of a better word, but the best of them are truly works of art and should be considered as such. The exquisite dolls featured in this book fall into the "fine art" category, and they and their makers deserve recognition in the art world.

Of course, an object need not be beautiful to be an exceptional work of art. There are many bizarre and wonderful character dolls created for adults that are not considered beautiful in the conventional sense, yet are remarkable artworks. What all these dolls have in common is that they evoke strong emotions in us. Whether they remind us of the grace and elegance of times long past, make us recall our own childhoods and children, raise our awareness of the beauty of other races and cultures, or call attention to the ills of our own society, they reach out to us in a very personal way.

menting with it.

A large number of the dolls that exist today are made of a combination of materials. For instance, a doll may have a china head and a cloth body with arms and legs fashioned from china, leather, or wood. Similarly, you'll often find porcelain or vinyl heads, arms, and legs attached to cloth bodies. During the Golden Age of dollmaking, it was not at all unusual for one company to make only doll heads, which were then put on bodies purchased from another company. Also, during the nineteenth century and early part of the twentieth, dolls' heads, and sometimes their limbs, were sold separately—not only to other companies, but also to members of the general public, who then made their own bodies and assembled the dolls in their homes.

Because a doll's head requires the most artistry and is what gives the doll its individual personality, when a doll is described as a wooden or a wax or a bisque, it means that the doll's head is made from that material, not that the entire doll is wood or wax or bisque. Of course, there are dolls made completely of one material. When this is the case, the word "all" is generally included in the description. Thus, an all-wood doll has not just a wood head, but also a wood body, arms, and legs.

While antiques are generally thought of as items that are at least 100 years old, that's not the case in the world of dolls. Doll collectors and dealers refer to dolls made prior to 1940 as antiques.

TERMINOLOGY

Very early representations of the human form were crudely carved from bone, wood, or alabaster. Later dolls were made of paper, cloth, leather, composition, ceramic, celluloid, or metal. In the 1940s, when hard plastic became widely used, it quickly found its way into the doll and toy industry. Next came the sculpting media: Sculpey, Fimo, and Cernit. Then, just a few years ago, Paperclay burst onto the scene and many dollmakers began experi-

WOODENS

Wood has been used for dolls throughout recorded history. It is readily available, easily worked, and considerably more durable than other media. Because of this, the variety of dolls crafted from wood runs the gamut from simply fashioned twig figures and crudely carved images to beautifully detailed, painted, and wigged creations.

According to Dorothy S., Elizabeth A., and Evelyn J.

Coleman's two-volume *Collector's Encyclopedia of Dolls*, in the seventeenth and eighteenth centuries the major areas of wood-doll production were Sonneberg, Oberammergau, Berchtesgaden, and Grödner Tal. Wood carving had been a cottage industry in these rich forest regions of Germany and Austria since the early sixteenth century, providing occupation for the peasants during the long winter months. By the 1700s carved and turned wood dolls in Germany were being mass-produced; until the latter part of the century, however, German trade guilds did not permit turners to paint their own works, so the dolls were shipped elsewhere for finishing.

While it was the German carvers and turners who produced the largest numbers of wood dolls during the seventeenth and eighteenth centuries, it is the English woodens that are best documented. In 1992 Bunny Campione, head of Campione Fine Arts of London and formerly of Sotheby's London auction house and creator of its doll department, tracked down twenty-two English woodens believed to date from the latter part of the seventeenth century. (Two of these dolls were featured at Sotheby's London May 14–15, 1992, auction.) After considerable research, Campione wrote an article for the June/July 1992 issue of *Dolls: The Collector's Magazine* in which she explored the idea that all these examples may have been created by the same person. Photographs of nine of the twenty-two dolls (including the two best-known examples, Lord and Lady Clapham, which are in the collection of London's Victoria and Albert Museum) were published with her article, and their resemblance is remarkable. All have similarly carved heads with nailed-on flax or real-hair wigs; round, rouged faces; Mona Lisa–type mouths; and thin, arched brows. Seven of the nine have painted eyes. The painted bodies of these dolls are also similar; they have identical peg jointing, padded upper arms, wood wrists and hands with long splayed fingers, and rather crudely shaped legs ending in block feet.

One finds more variety among the eighteenth-century English woodens. Some of these dolls have round faces

A thirteen-inch-high English wooden doll, circa 1800 (By kind permission of Sotheby's London)

similar to their predecessors, but others have more realistically shaped heads with attractive oval faces. Painted eyes became less common during this century, being replaced with dark-colored, pupilless glass eyes. The head and torso of these dolls are generally one piece, but the torso shapes vary. Some are quite curvaceous, having tiny waists, wide hips, and carved buttocks; others are square or conical. There are also differences in the attention given to the legs of the eighteenth-century woodens.

Some have smooth upper legs that are jointed at the knees and shapely lower legs with carved calves, ankle bones, and feet. Others have crudely carved straight legs and triangular-shaped feet with no indication of toes. Because the dolls with well-carved heads and torsos are not always those with beautifully shaped legs and feet, one suspects that more than one carver worked on each doll.

Wood dolls continued to be made in England, Germany, and other European countries throughout the nineteenth and twentieth centuries. There are many charming folk art dolls made of wood, and a handful of today's well-known doll artists work in wood. Unfortunately, during the nineteenth century, the quality of wood dolls, particularly those made in England, declined. This was no doubt due to two factors: the Industrial Revolution and dollmakers' mastery of other media. With the Industrial Revolution came a rising middle class that wanted goods similar to those of the wealthy, but at lower prices. To meet the demand, dollmakers, ceramicists, and other artisans stepped up production and paid less attention to the details that made the earlier and more expensive works so lovely. At the same time, interest in wood dolls was fading as beautiful wax and china dolls became more available and popular.

Perhaps the most famous name to emerge in the wood-doll industry during the early part of the twentieth century is the American firm A. Schoenhut & Company of Philadelphia. The company was founded in 1872 by a German immigrant, Albert Schoenhut, who came from a long line of woodworkers; his grandfather Anton, and his father, Frederick, had both carved wood dolls in Germany. The Schoenhut company initially made children's musical toys, at which it was relatively successful. But the company's claim to fame came after the 1903 introduction of its Humpty Dumpty Circus, which included its first dolls: a ringmaster, clowns, and acrobats. Not long after this Schoenhut devised a spring-jointing system for his dolls (the patent for it was filed in 1909) that enabled them to be positioned in a variety of lifelike poses. This, coupled with the realistic-looking faces of the early

models, made them highly popular. Most of these dolls are carved basswood; some have carved and painted hair, others have wigs. Schoenhut died in 1911, but his six sons carried on the business into the 1930s. Unfortunately, near the end of the company's existence, the quality of the dolls suffered. The early ones, however, are remarkable examples of the dollmakers' craft.

Today the seventeenth- and eighteenth-century woodens are highly prized by collectors, and the best examples bring five and even six figures at auctions and antique doll shows. On the other hand, prices for the Schoenhuts are much, much lower because they are fairly recent examples of wood dolls and not difficult to find. According to Barry Leo Delaney, a professional appraiser who tracks the antique doll market for *Dolls* magazine, nice examples of these American-made wood dolls can be bought for under $1,500, although the rarest might cost more.

WAXES

Carved wax figures date back to ancient times. The Greeks and Romans created portraits in wax, and the Romans also made wax dolls, as did centuries of Italians after the fall of the Roman Empire. By the fifteenth century life-size wax portraits were being made in Italy. The popularity of such figures spread across Europe and reached its pinnacle in England, where traveling exhibits and wax museums attracted all classes of people. The best known of these exhibits is the wax museum of Madame Tussaud, which opened in London in the early 1800s. Born and raised in France, Anna Marie Tussaud was adopted by Philippe Guillaume Mathé Curtius, a famous French wax modeler, after her mother went to work for him as his housekeeper. In *The History of Wax Dolls*, author Mary Hillier notes that while Curtius is often referred to as Tussaud's uncle, there was no blood relationship between the two, although Hillier hints that there might have been another kind of relationship be-

An eighteen-inch-high early-nineteenth-century English wax, unmarked but in the Pierotti style (By kind permission of Sotheby's London)

tween Curtius and Tussaud's mother. Whatever the case, it was from Curtius that Madame Tussaud learned her craft.

While fine examples of wax dolls dating from the seventeenth and eighteenth centuries can be found in museums and private collections, it was in the nineteenth century—after interest in wax figures was created by the public exhibition of life-size models—that wax dollmaking truly came into its own. The better nineteenth-century waxes are indeed charming. They have finely modeled features and a translucency and softness of color that more closely resembles skin tones than any of the earlier dolls and many of the later ones. Unfortunately, the very properties that make wax such an excellent medium for dollmaking—its malleability and the relatively low temperature required for it to liquefy—are also its biggest detriments; these dolls are easily scratched and marred, as well as damaged by temperature changes.

The most famous of the wax dollmakers were the Pierottis and Montanaris. As their names suggest, both families were Italian in origin; however, it was in England that they made their delightful wax dolls. The first doll-making member of the Pierotti family was Domenico, born in 1760. Domenico's father was a vintner; his mother was an Englishwoman whom his father presumably met while in England on business. Domenico was raised in Italy, but moved to England about 1780 and, like his father, took an Englishwoman for his bride. By 1793 he was selling dolls in London; it is believed that the dolls he offered were waxes that he modeled himself. Two of his sons, Henry and John, made dolls, but it was Henry's poured waxes that established the family as dollmakers extraordinaire.

Some of Henry Pierotti's dolls were modeled after his own children; others depicted the children of England's Queen Victoria. They were delicately colored with carmine and white lead, and many of his better examples were poured in two or three layers. The dolls' hair was inserted into the wax by single strands or in small clumps. The dolls' arms and legs were wax, and their fingernails and toenails were engraved. The cloth bodies, believed to have been made by the women in the family, were stuffed with cow hair. After Henry's death in 1871, his children and grandchildren carried on the family business until the 1920s.

The Montanari family's reputation as wax dollmakers was established in 1851 when Augusta Montanari won a prize at the Great Exhibition in London for her display of wax dolls. These dolls depicted adults and children of all ages, including examples modeled on England's royal family as well as children from America and Africa. When

Augusta and her husband, Napoleon, began modeling wax dolls is vague, but Napoleon appears to have been working as a wax modeler in the late 1840s. It is a shame that the Montanaris didn't date their dolls, as so many of today's doll artists do; it would have made the researcher's job so much easier! Still, at least the Montanaris signed a great many of theirs.

Napoleon Montanari was born in Corsica in 1813; Augusta was an Englishwoman, born in 1818. While their name is the best known of all wax dollmakers, there is scant record of their personal lives. Their eldest son, Richard, also a wax dollmaker, was born in New York in 1840, so the couple obviously were in the United States at that time. Also, one suspects that they had visited Mexico, as some of their dolls depict Mexicans. After Augusta's death in 1864, her husband and son carried on the family business.

In the early nineteenth century, while the English wax dollmakers were honing their skills, the Germans were busily creating religious figures in wax. However, inspired by the English dolls displayed at the international exhibition held in London in 1851, they turned their talents to making poured wax dolls, and just a few years later were exporting their creations to countries around the world. The German wax doll industry was centered in Sonneberg, a town in the eastern German region of Thuringia, and wax dolls were made there until the 1930s. Unfortunately, as little is known about the individual German wax dollmakers as is known about the German carvers who created so many of the woodens.

By the early twentieth century the heyday of wax dolls was past. Still, some of the most beautiful wax ladies come from this period. They are the Lafitte Désirat figures created in France from about 1902 to 1920. Although these wax-headed figures are not dolls in the true sense—they were designed to display the fashions of the times rather than for play—they hold an important place in the history of dolls. The dolls are named for the two sisters who designed and created them, Augusta Daussat Désirat and Louise Daussat Lafitte, although how much input

they had on the figures' wax heads is unknown as the heads are believed to have been made at the Musée de Grevin. The figures are remarkable, not only for their beauty but also for the record they provide on women's clothing during the first two decades of the twentieth century.

A sad footnote in the history of wax dollmaking is the fate suffered by many of the modelers, including Henry Pierotti's son, Charles Pierotti: early death caused by lead poisoning. Coloring agents used for the wax dolls included white lead and lead chromate; at the time, no one understood the inherent dangers of working with these toxic mixtures.

PAPIER-MÂCHÉS

In the early part of the nineteenth century, when modelers in England were creating beautiful wax dolls, German toy makers were discovering the potential of papier-mâché as a medium for dolls. Papier-mâché was not new; it had been used for dolls made in France during the sixteenth century, and by German dollmakers in the eighteenth century. However, it was after 1815, when a method of producing metal molds was invented in France, that papier-mâché doll heads were mass-produced. According to *The German Doll Encyclopedia: 1800–1939* by Jürgen and Marianne Cieslik, Johann Friedrich Müller was the first Sonneberg factory owner to produce such molded doll heads. He began making them about 1820; later, many other dollmakers produced them, including Johann Daniel Kestner, Jr., of Waltershausen, another Thuringian town.

The German makers experimented with many mixtures for papier-mâché, as well as with coatings for these doll heads, some of which were dipped in wax or had wax poured over them to give them a more natural look. By the middle of the nineteenth century, papier-mâché dolls were at the height of their popularity. The dolls were lightweight and inexpensive, and the best examples rivaled the waxes and chinas in beauty. They were being made not just in Germany, but also in other European countries and in the United States, where one papier-mâché dollmaker, Ludwig Greiner of Philadelphia, obtained what is believed to be the first United States patent for a doll's head. By the 1870s the popularity of papier-mâché dolls began to wane, as porcelain bisques became all the rage. However, about that time papier-mâché became a popular medium for jointed dolls' bodies, and it continued to be used for bodies into the twentieth century.

PORCELAINS

In the early 1700s, Thuringia became the center for porcelain production because of the large concentrations of certain types of clay there. When the start of the Industrial Revolution in the mid-1700s created a huge market for what were then considered luxury items, such as decorative objects, the German porcelain factories quickly responded to this demand. Initially producing figurines and the like, dolls were a natural addition to their output. By the beginning of the nineteenth century, porcelain had become popular as a material for making dolls. One of the first porcelain factories in Thuringia to create dolls was that of Kestner & Company, founded in 1805 by Johannes Daniel Kestner, Jr., in Waltershausen. This establishment remained in operation until the 1930s when it merged with another German firm, Kämmer & Reinhardt. Kestner's work was highly regarded in its day, and still is by collectors. Porcelain retained its popularity with dollmakers until the middle of the twentieth century when "unbreakable" materials, such as composition and plastic, became the standard.

Chinas

Glazed porcelain dolls, referred to as chinas, existed in the early 1800s, but they became popular in the 1840s and were made in vast quantities until about 1940. The early chinas were expensive toys, but soon they were being produced at prices that the middle classes could afford. The majority of them come from Germany, but there are marked examples made by Denmark's Royal Copenhagen Manufactury and by Jacob Petit of France. Unfortunately, few of the German-made chinas are marked, although there are rare examples bearing the Meissen mark, and some early and lovely ones carry the initials K.P.M., the mark of Königliche Porzellan Manufaktur.

When one talks about chinas, for the most part one is referring to dolls with china heads and, perhaps, china arms and legs. There are some all-china dolls, but the majority do not have china bodies. Some, particularly those dating from the 1840s, have peg-wood bodies, but bodies constructed of cloth or leather are more common. Some of these bodies were commercially made, but prior to 1880 most china heads and limbs were sold separately, and the bodies for them were fashioned by the dolls' first owners.

A twenty-inch-high unmarked German china, circa 1875-80

Most of the pre-1880s chinas were made by pressing damp clay into molds; when the clay had dried to the desired hardness, it was removed from the mold, cleaned, and fired. Later dolls were made by pouring slip into molds; when enough of the slip had set, the remainder was poured out. The mold was then removed, and the clay was cleaned and fired. One can tell which method was used by looking into the doll's head. The interiors of pressed heads are a bit rough, while the poured ones are smooth. The color of the china dolls varies from stark white to cream to a pinkish flesh tone, often referred to as pink luster. China heads generally have rouged cheeks and painted features; however, some have glass eyes and a rare few have sleep eyes, which are glass eyes covered by a lid that opens and closes. Most chinas have molded and painted hair, but wigged versions are also found.

Chinas are generally identified by their hairdos, and so distinct and lovely are some of these coifs that earlier generations of collectors have given them names. Some of these styles are descriptive, such as lowbrow (the hair is parted in the center and covers much of the doll's forehead; this hairdo is found on many of the chinas produced from the late 1880s to 1930), flattop, or highbrow (a center-parted hairdo that leaves much of the forehead showing). Other styles were named for famous people, such as Mary Todd Lincoln, Jenny Lind (known as the Swedish Nightingale), and opera singer Adelina Patti. By the 1860s chinas' hairdos were being adorned with molded flowers, leaves, combs, bows, and snoods, or partly covered by molded hats. In addition to decorating the chinas' hair, some manufacturers decorated the dolls' shoulder plates with molded necklaces or the tops of blouses complete with collars, pleats, or ruffles. All this adds a great variety to the chinas and helps historians date them, although one can only assume approximate dates for individual dolls because any one style may have been made over a period of twenty years or more.

Considering that chinas are easily broken, a surprising number exist today. As prices for the woodens and waxes escalate, more antique doll collectors are discovering the charm and beauty of the chinas. Still, prices for these lovely antiques are reasonable; one can find nice examples for just a few hundred dollars. Of course, the rarer ones are costlier, generally more than $1,000. The most unusual, all-original examples start at $3,000 and may go for more than $10,000, although prices above $5,000 are unusual. What's rare? The very early chinas and those with unusual hairdos, such as buns or coronet braids. Those depicting men and boys are also rare. Because few boys' heads were made, it's not unusual to find girl dolls with short hair dressed as boys. Also rare are chinas with painted brown eyes (most painted eyes were blue) or sleep eyes, and chinas with brown hair (most early chinas had black hair, while blond hair is not uncommon for later examples). The quality of the workmanship also plays a role in determining price, as does the dolls' skin tone, with the pink-luster coloring being sought after by collectors.

French and German Bisques

When one thinks of antique dolls, the image that usually comes to mind is that of chubby-faced porcelain-bisque dolls with wide-open staring glass eyes and long blond Mary Pickford curls. Dolls such as these were created during the 1875–1930 Golden Age of dollmaking. Although so many different types of dolls have been made, it is these porcelain bisques that are the cornerstone of antique doll collecting, and the majority of serious collectors will have at least one in their possession. By far, today's most desirable antique dolls were produced during this era. France and Germany were the dominant producers of bisque dolls during the Golden Age of dollmaking. Although England and Japan also produced some bisques, their creations were well below the standards set by France and Germany. In terms of volume, Germany dominated, and their bisques are most commonly found today. In terms of quality, France reigned, and many of their dolls are the most sought after (with the notable exception of the German J. D. Kestner firm, whose dolls have been compared to those of the French).

When collectors use the term "bisque," they are speaking of porcelain dolls that have been fired in a kiln twice, with color added between firings. Traditionally, after a porcelain doll part was removed from its mold, it was fired. This unpainted fired piece was referred to as "biscuitware," or bisque. These pieces were then tinted and painted and fired again to create porcelain-bisque dolls.

The procedure was expensive, but if the dolls were produced in mass quantities, as they generally were, a profit could be generated. Bisques were made from about 1850 until 1930. The earliest dolls tend to be simple. Their heads and shoulders were made as one piece; they had molded hair, molded eyes, and closed mouths. In time, the various doll manufacturers experimented with different techniques. They created heads that turned on necks; they added wigs, inset glass eyes, and later sleep eyes; they molded open mouths, sometimes with teeth and tongues.

Fashionable Lady Dolls

The first bisque doll heads produced were made in Germany. These heads were used to make complete dolls in Germany, as well as exported to France where they were also assembled into dolls, using bodies and clothing manufactured there. In the mid-1800s the French doll manufacturers were primarily known for their doll bodies, particularly those of kid leather, and their doll clothing. (Although the making of bisque doll heads was, for the most part, neglected in France at this time, there were some establishments that did manufacture them, including Jumeau and Bru. These early heads, however, were not up to the quality of the later French bisque heads.) France's German-headed dolls were dressed in haute-couture French fashions. The majority of the early bisques were lady dolls, and while they were created primarily as playthings, they were also used to show off the latest styles. In an article in an 1869 edition of *Harper's Bazaar*, the author stated, "The chief French toy is a doll, not a representation of an infant . . . but a model of a lady attired in the height of fashion." These fashionable lady dolls were at the peak of their popularity from the 1860s until around 1885. Frequently referred to as fashion dolls or sometimes Parisiennes, they are prized by collectors today, and those with French heads, and, naturally, original clothing are highly sought after.

The Bébé

Among the French companies that produced bisque doll heads was the one founded in Paris in 1842 by Pierre François Jumeau, who was determined to make France the center of the world's doll industry. According to antique expert Helen Nolan, Jumeau was the leading French dollmaker from the 1860s through the first decade of the twentieth century; it made more dolls than any other producer in France. During the first years of the company's existence it was known primarily for its kid bodies and doll clothing. The jury at the first International Exhibition in 1851 awarded Jumeau a First Place

A twenty-two-inch-high French child doll by Casimir Bru, circa 1890, marked "Bru Jne R"

Medal for its exhibit, but commented, "The dolls on which these dresses are displayed present no point worthy of commendation, but the dresses themselves are very beautiful." Gradually the firm began to receive recognition for its bisque heads. However, it wasn't until Pierre retired and his son Émile took over the firm in the late 1870s, and the world-renowned Bébé Jumeau was "born," that the Jumeau name became synonymous with quality dolls.

The bébé was different from the bisque dolls that had been produced to that date because it had the idealized features of a child. (It is said that the inspiration for the bébé face came from a portrait of four-year-old Henri IV of France.) These doll heads—with large glass eyes that look like miniature paperweights, curly, long-haired wigs, and rosy cheeks—were usually placed on jointed composition or wood bodies. They were dressed in outfits of satin, taffeta, silk, lace, and ribbons that were accessorized with elaborate undergarments, hats, shoes, stockings, and jewelry.

The bébés were instantly popular and were soon manufactured by all the French companies. A major competitor of Jumeau's was Bru Jne. & Cie., founded by Casimir Bru Jeune (Junior) in Paris in 1866. Although many of the Brus, particularly the earliest bébés, are of the same caliber as the Jumeaux, the quality of the Brus is not consistent.

The Germans, in competition for their share of the market, came up with their own version of the bébé, which is referred to by collectors as the dolly-face doll. The dolly-faced dolls were produced in much greater quantities than the French bébés. One of the main producers of dolly-face heads, and of bisque heads in general, was the firm of Armand Marseille. This entrepreneur emigrated to Thuringia from Russia and, in 1885, bought an already existing porcelain factory in Sonne-

---

A twenty-six-inch French poured bisque by Jumeau, circa 1885, marked "12" (By kind permission of Sotheby's London)

berg. Although Marseille only began making doll heads in 1890, rather late when compared to the other firms of the time, this prolific German factory produced a multitude of heads for companies in Europe and America. Its most popular was the open-mouth, smiling dolly-face head. Among the other major German companies to successfully manufacture these doll heads were Simon & Halbig and J. D. Kestner.

A rare, fifteen-inch-high oriental toddler by J.D. Kestner, circa 1900-05, marked "Made in Germany 10//J.D.K. 243"

The Character Dolls

Around the turn of the century, a trend developed in Germany in reaction to the idealized dolly and bébé faces: artists began sculpting dolls with more realistic features. Although these dolls hardly convey the realism found in many of the artists' creations of today, the idea behind these "character dolls," according to renowned doll expert Jan Foulke, was to create a doll that looked real, like an actual child. One of the first German firms to register Character Dolls as a trade name was Kämmer & Reinhardt in 1909. This manufacturer, founded by doll designer Ernst Kämmer and salesman Franz Reinhardt in 1886 in Waltershausen, manufactured only doll bodies. The dolls they sold were created using heads made to their specifications by other factories. Simon & Halbig was the prime manufacturer for their character heads.

Once the trend caught on other German manufacturers began creating character dolls, and soon there were dolls that frowned, pouted, cried, smiled, laughed, flirted, or looked serene. The heads were usually found on composition bodies with ball joints for easy posing. In a turnaround, the French began copying the Germans and made their own versions of character dolls. The popularity of the character children lasted only about ten years, and these bisque dolls are now more difficult to find than other types. The popularity of the character babies, such as Armand Marseille's "My Dream Baby," lasted a bit longer, reaching a peak in the 1920s.

The S.F.B.J.

Due to the popularity of the German dolls, and the large quantities created and exported to countries throughout the world, including France. the French doll industry was faced with a real threat. In 1916 the French magazine *Gazette des Beaux Arts* noted, "The Germans had ruined the French doll industry in a few years by methodically copying and underselling." In response to this situation, in 1899, ten companies banded together to form the Société Française de Fabrication des Bébés et Jouets (French Society for the Manufacture of Dolls and Toys), popularly known by its initials S.F.B.J. Most of the joining firms were French, including Jumeau, Bru, and Rabery & Delphieu, but some were German, notably Fleischmann & Bloedel, one of the largest stockholders. The quality of the dolls produced by the S.F.B.J. was

good, but never rose to the level previously found in the dolls of its highest quality partners, Jumeau and Bru.

During and after World War I, the German doll industry fell on hard times due to shortages of supplies and anti-German sentiment. This left an opening that the S.F.B.J. stepped in and filled. The organization prospered and, for a while, put France on top as a doll producer.

THE BEGINNING OF THE MODERN ERA

The majority of the German porcelain factories were located in rural and remote areas of the country, where labor and other costs were low. French firms, on the other hand, were located in or near cities, where operating costs were much higher. This allowed the German companies to produce quality dolls in larger quantities and for less money than the French. Until the start of World War I, the majority of little girls worldwide played with German bisques. In the 1930s and 1940s, when the hobby of doll collecting was in its infancy in the United States, most collectors started out with the German bisques, as those were the dolls of their childhood.

The Golden Age of bisque dolls began to fade with the use of celluloid, which was extremely cheap to produce in the early years of the twentieth century, and with composition, which was developed in 1850 but only became widely used in dollmaking after the turn of the century. With the beginning of World War II, the Golden Age came to an abrupt end. After the war was over, plastic emerged as a new dollmaking medium, completely altering the industry. Although Germany never recovered the place it held prior to World War I, it continued to play an important role into the twentieth century, along with an important newcomer, the United States. The S.F.B.J. and other French firms continued producing dolls into the 1950s, but never with the same prominence as during the Golden Age.

YESTERDAY AND TODAY

So many fascinating and talented people have contributed to the rich history of dolls that it seems wrong to focus on just a few. However, when one thinks of dollmaking in the first half of the twentieth century, four names stand out: Käthe Kruse of Germany, Elena Scavini of Italy, Sasha Morgenthaler of Switzerland, and Beatrice Alexander Behrman of the United States. Each of these women made dolls designed for play, although they were coveted by adults as well, and became known worldwide. These four women laid the foundations for contemporary dollmakers to be recognized as creative artists.

Käthe Kruse

Käthe Kruse, née Katherina Simon, was born in Breslau, Germany, in 1883. Her unmarried mother eked out a living as a seamstress, managing to house, feed, and clothe herself and her young daughter, but unable to afford any of life's luxuries. One of young Käthe's few divertissements was provided by an aunt and uncle who took her on monthly excursions to the theater. Fascinated by the performances she saw, Käthe decided on a career as an actress. At age sixteen she had her first speaking role in a Breslau theater production; by the time she was eighteen, she had signed a contract with the Lessing Theater of Berlin, where she performed under the name Hedda Somin. Obviously talented, she was soon offered good roles not only in Berlin, but in Warsaw and Moscow. She received critical acclaim and made more money than she'd ever imagined possible, money that she shared with her mother, whom she brought to Berlin.

At the turn of the century Berlin was a fast-growing city and the center of the arts in Germany. One can imagine what a heady experience it was for an eighteen-year-old, raised in near-poverty, to be a successful part of the city's artistic community. Among the artists she met was Max Kruse, a noted sculptor; though he was thirty years older than she, the two became close friends and lovers. Soon Käthe became pregnant, but she refused to marry Max. Their first child, Maria (nicknamed Mimerle) was born in December 1902. When Käthe became pregnant with their second child, Max convinced her to quit acting and move to Switzerland, where their second daughter, Sophie (nicknamed Fifi), was born in 1904. During this time Max maintained his studio in Berlin, so the couple had long periods of separation. However, Käthe was not alone with her children; her mother accompanied them to Switzerland and lived there until her death in 1906.

It was Mimerle's request for a doll that she could care for in the same way her mother cared for Fifi that led to Käthe's first attempt at dollmaking. Käthe asked Max to buy a doll for Mimerle in Berlin, but he wrote back saying that all the dolls he found were "ugly, stiff, and cold." He refused to buy any of these dolls, instead suggesting that Käthe make one herself. Thus, in 1905, she made her first doll. It was a simple creation, made out of cloth, filled with sand, and had a potato for its face; but Mimerle loved it because it had the weight of a real baby and was soft and cuddly. Of course, this doll did not have a long life as its potato head rotted and its seams leaked sand. So Käthe looked for other ways and means of making dolls, experimenting over the next five years until she developed a realistic-looking child doll that could withstand a youngster's rough play. The doll had a hand-painted molded cloth face and a cloth body filled with wood shavings; later dolls were stuffed with reindeer hair.

Not all Käthe's time was devoted to experimenting with doll design, however. Between 1905 and 1910 she and Max traveled extensively, living in various European cities. Also, Käthe had two more children, a son who died at birth and a daughter, Hanne, who was born in 1909. It was also in 1909 that Käthe finally agreed to marry Max. At the time she was 26 years old and he 55. During the following years they had four more children: Michael, Jochen, Friedebald, and Max.

In 1910, when Käthe and Max were once again living

in Berlin, she was invited to display her dolls at the Home-made Toys Exhibition sponsored by Berlin's Hermann Tietz department store. Her cloth children, so radically different from the chinas and bisques of the day, created a sensation, and her career as a dollmaker began in earnest. The German firm of Kämmer & Reinhardt acquired the rights to produce her dolls; however, unhappy with the quality of the manufactured dolls, Käthe bought back the rights to her design. Shortly thereafter she got an order for 150 dolls from the American toy store F. A. O. Schwarz. Having no production facilities, she frantically made these dolls in her home. The ensuing chaos made Käthe and Max realize the need for her to have a separate work space. In 1912 they moved to Bad Kösen and opened a workshop where Käthe produced dolls, with the help of a growing work force, until 1950. A shrewd businesswoman, Käthe Kruse continued to improve her dolls—adding real-hair wigs, jointed limbs, and swivel heads—and to create new designs. Also, she expanded her market, exporting her dolls to other countries, including England, Sweden, and The Netherlands.

While Käthe Kruse's reputation as a dollmaker grew and her business flourished, the war years took their toll. She lost two of her sons, Jochen and Friedebald; also, in 1942, her husband died. At the end of the war, when Germany was divided, her two remaining sons, Max and Michael, left Bad Kösen (which was in the Soviet Zone) for the West and founded workshops in Donauwörth and Bad Pyrmonth. Several years later these workshops were merged in Donauwörth. In 1950 Käthe Kruse escaped from East Germany, as did some of her employees, and joined her sons. She was active in the business until the mid-1950s, after which it was headed by three of her children, Max, Michael, and Hanne, plus Hanne's husband, Heinz Adler. The workshop was incorporated as Käthe Kruse Puppen GmbH in 1958. Käthe Kruse died

Two seventeen-inch-high Käthe Kruse Doll I Red Ridinghoods, 1913

on January 10, 1968. However, members of her family remained active in the company until 1990, when it was purchased by Stephen and Andrea Christenson and the family of Prince Albrecht zu Castell-Castell. Her dolls continue to be made in Donauwörth, using production methods similar to those established by Käthe Kruse in the early days. Ironically, these dolls, designed so specifically as "a child for the child," are now more sought after by adult collectors than by children.

Elena Scavini

Elena Scavini (née Elena von Konig) was born in 1886 in Turin, Italy, where her father, a German chemistry professor, was serving as director of the Regia Stazione Agraria. During Elena's early years the family had a comfortable life, but that changed in 1893 when her father died leaving her mother with five children to support. According to an article by Shirley Buchholz in the Summer 1980 issue of *Doll News* (published by the United Federation of Doll Clubs), Elena's mother was a skilled pianist and multilingual, so was able to earn a living by giving piano and language lessons. The family lived in Turin until the turn of the century, when Elena's mother accepted a job as an interpreter in Lausanne. Elena accompanied her mother to Switzerland, where she got the first of a series of jobs teaching language as her mother had done.

Interested in art and photography, she moved to Düsseldorf, Germany, in 1906 to study these subjects. Her stay there was interrupted by trips to Italy, and then ended when war broke out. Italian by birth, but living in the German homeland of her father, 28-year-old Elena must have been torn as to where her loyalties lay. Given a choice on where to live, she decided to return to Italy, undoubtedly influenced by her love for Italian artist Enrico Scavini. In 1915 she and Enrico were married; soon, Elena became pregnant and gave birth to a daughter, who died shortly thereafter. Then in 1918 thirty-year-old Enrico joined the Italian armed forces as an aviator.

A very rare, twenty-two-inch-high Lenci Oriental Lady, circa 1920s

Left alone in Turin, Elena began making dolls in order to supplement her husband's meager military pay. According to her autobiography, these dolls were born out of her profound grief at having lost her little daughter. She named her first doll "Lencina," which is the diminutive form of Lenci, the nickname by which Elena was known.

Elena's first dolls, fashioned at her family's apartment with the help of her brother, Bubine Konig, were made of felt and had steam-pressed faces and flesh-colored arms and legs. Exactly why she used felt is unknown. It may have been that, since Turin was a cloth-producing center, fine woolen felt was readily available during the war years when so many other products were scarce. However, one must remember that Elena was living in Ger-

many when Käthe Kruse's cloth dolls were introduced and received wide acclaim. Also, the famous German firm of Steiff had manufactured felt-headed dolls since 1894, and Elena must have had some familiarity with them. Whatever the reason, Elena Scavini's felt dolls were remarkable, and those produced during the first few decades of her career are among the finest cloth dolls ever made.

When Enrico returned from the war, he joined Elena in what was becoming a lucrative dollmaking business. In 1919 the company was officially founded in Turin, and its trademark, "Ludus Est Nobis Constanter Industria" ("To Play Is Our Constant Work") was registered. This motto was written in a circle around a child's spinning top, and the first letter of each word (which, when connected, spell Lenci) was capitalized. Also in 1919, Enrico applied for a United States patent for the process by which the felt heads were pressed. At this time the Scavinis were still making the dolls in their apartment, and Elena was doing all the design work. But by 1920 a number of other artists had joined the firm; among them was Sandro Vacchetti, a painter who later became Lenci's art director.

The Scavinis were almost instantly successful. In 1921 they were already offering more than 100 different characters, including children of various nationalities. By 1922 their dolls were being exported around the world, and the couple moved their operation to a factory on Turin's Via Marco Polo. That same year the company began marketing their dolls under the Lenci name (prior to this, the dolls were marketed as "Scavini Dolls" or as "Lenci di E. Scavini"). The majority of the Lenci dolls depict children; they have mohair wigs and expressive faces, often with side-glancing eyes. Great attention was paid to the dolls' costumes, which were made of felt and organdy, often adorned with embroidery and appliquéd felt. These dolls were designed for children, but were never inexpensive, and advertisements for them stressed their artistic design and the amount of handwork that went into their construction.

By 1923 Lenci also offered boudoir dolls, which were

especially popular in America. According to a 1923 *Toys and Novelties* article, the craze for these dolls was not limited to women: "Many men," it says, "were among the purchasers generally favoring the sophisticated French chorus girls, legs crossed, with a cigarette tilted at an angle." Lenci's boudoir dolls were among the most elaborate of the 1920s and 1930s art dolls. Unlike the Lenci dolls depicting children, these exotic ladies, Pierrots, Pierrettes, and depictions of movie stars (such as Rudolph Valentino) were not intended for play. The company considered them decorative objects and advertised them as such; one ad, which appeared in a 1923 issue of *Playthings* magazine, read, "Buy a Lenci doll to place on a hassock, to lend color to your boudoir, to decorate a corner of your limousine." And that's just what Americans did, for few of the Lenci boudoir dolls that exist today show signs of play.

As Lenci's reputation grew, many more young and innovative artists joined the firm. By the late 1920s the Scavinis had moved to another factory and were employing more than 800 people. In addition to dolls, Lenci produced felt animals, wooden accessories for the dolls, clothing for children, pillows, wall hangings, tablecloths, napkins, even ceramic objects. Then, in 1937 the Scavinis gave up control of the firm and their trademark to the brothers Pilade and Flavio Garella. Both the Garellas had joined Lenci in 1933; Pilade managed the commercial side of the business, and Flavio was the head of production. Enrico left the firm in 1937 and died in 1938; Elena served as art director until 1941. The following year Pilade Garella's son, Beppe, joined the firm, eventually heading it. Beppe Garella died in 1992, but Lenci continues today to make felt dolls under the leadership of Beppe's daughter, Blandina (known as Bibija).

Elena Scavini, who became known worldwide as "Madame Lenci," died in 1974. Her extraordinary felt dolls live on in collections around the world, serving as a testament to her artistic talent and what she often described as the secret to her success: "One must always use extremely good taste."

A nineteen-inch-high gypsum-head BII Sasha, circa 1940s, all original except for shoes

Sasha Morgenthaler

Sasha Morgenthaler lent her name to wistful, almost lonely looking dolls that mirrored her soul; dolls that she hoped aroused "feelings of approval, love, and humanity," she wrote in her autobiography. Eventually mass-produced by a British firm for twenty years, the Sasha dolls, unfortunately, have not been manufactured since 1986. This, however, in no way diminishes the impact of these dolls and their maker, or the importance they hold with collectors today.

The artist was born to Marie and Edward von Sinner on November 30, 1893, in Bern, Switzerland. For the most part ignored by her busy, emancipated mother, who spent a great amount of time in the company of artists and intellectuals, young Sasha was raised by governesses and servants. She faked a weak heart and withdrew into her own world of make-believe. As the child of artistically and musically inclined parents, and surrounded by the arts, it's no surprise she filled her world with her own sculptures and paintings.

One of her mother's friends was the painter Paul Klee, who, luckily for Sasha, recognized her talents early on in a way her own parents did not. In 1910, at the arrangement of Klee, she left home to attend an art academy in Geneva and later studied with the Swiss traditional painter Cuno Amiet in Oschwand. Sasha was very influenced by Klee, who was part of the Blaue Reiter (Blue Rider) movement, and her art reflects this influence. The Blaue Reiter manifesto called on artists to express not only what they saw, but what they felt. They felt artists should draw on artistic traditions in folk art, ancient and primitive art, even children's drawing. In general, they believed any means of expression was worthwhile. This declaration was taken to heart by Sasha, whose dolls, although simple-looking and created for play, carry tremendous emotional appeal.

While in Oschwand, Sasha met painter Ernst Morgenthaler, whom she married in 1916. By 1924 she was the mother of three children and was busy creating stuffed animals, rag dolls, and puppets for them to play with. (Klee fashioned fanciful puppets for his young son's amusement, and it is thought that those creations may have led Sasha to create hand puppets for her own children.) She didn't want to buy any of the dolls being sold at that time because she felt they represented an artificial way of life. Eventually she turned to sculpting, but it wasn't until 1939 that any of her work was displayed publicly. Her first pieces to be exhibited were mannequins, which were displayed at the Swiss National Exposition in Zurich. This display marked a turning point in the artist's career, as they brought her public recognition as a sculptor.

The start of World War II temporarily put an end to Sasha's artistic activities. In order to do her part during the war, the artist organized the Hülfstrupp, a branch of the civilian Women's Auxiliary Corps in Zurich. The women who served in the Hülfstrupp were trained to organize and carry out the evacuation of the civilian population in case of an invasion of Switzerland. They also put their training to use in aiding refugee groups, mainly women and children, who came through Zurich during the war. The Hülfstrupp would meet the refugees in the train station and see to it that they were fed and cared for until taken in by Swiss families. In an attempt to bring smiles to the sad faces of these children, Sasha began to make dolls for them. Creating the dolls also helped to ease her own pain at what was happening. "I was trying to make my dreams come true," the artist wrote in her autobiography, "and became very happy when I was able to make dolls with a human appearance that the children could love. This lifelike appearance comes from the non-symmetrical proportions that form a unity and, therefore, become the base of a lot of expression possibilities!"

In 1941 Sasha entered and won first prize in a toy competition held by the Swiss government. The result was a multitude of orders for life-size puppets. After creating puppets, marionettes, and mannequins for several years, Sasha began experimenting with making dolls in various media. She put together a team of craftspeople to help her create what she felt would be the perfect doll. She tried and discarded wood, wax, and plaster and finally decided upon a synthetic resin, a forerunner of hard plastic, as being the best material for the dolls' heads. The expression she settled on was a wistful, almost perplexed demeanor. She did not want her dolls to have the ingratiating smiles painted on the dolls of the time because she felt that didn't accurately reflect the mood of children. She wanted her dolls to become their little owners' friends.

At the Sasha Museum, located in the artist's former town house in Zurich, there is a filmed interview with Sasha in which she explains that she wanted her dolls to represent children from all over the world, of every race and every color, privileged and underprivileged, from country or city, to "arouse feelings of understanding, love, and compassion." The artist traveled the world photographing and sketching children and their clothing so that she could accurately portray their very different lives. Regardless of the type of children her dolls portrayed, they all had the same sad, pensive expression that Sasha felt captured the universal difficulty of growing up.

Sasha had hoped her works would replace the dolls found on toy shop shelves, which she felt were vacuous and meaningless (except for the Käthe Kruse dolls, which she admired). Although she wanted to make her dolls more available and affordable than others, by the 1950s she was producing only 250 a year in her studio. Her dolls were just too expensive to be toys and ended up being collector's items. This led her, after the death of her husband in 1963, to try having the Sashas mass-produced despite her fear that the dolls would lose their human expression. A German company produced them in 1964, but not being satisfied, Sasha put an end to production after one year.

A year later the artist met John and Sara Doggart, who owned the British firm Frido Ltd. They were looking for a special doll to produce for children, and the Sasha doll was just what they wanted. Hesitant, the artist worked closely with them until, she said in her autobiography, "It became possible to make dolls that fulfilled my dreams." Unfortunately, upon their retirement in 1986 the Doggarts were not able to find someone to take over production of the Sasha dolls. However, Sasha Morgenthaler was not to know of this. She had died in February 1975 believing that her dream of creating affordable, endearing dolls capable of sharing a child's lonely moments had been fulfilled.

Madame Alexander

Undoubtedly, the first lady of dolls in the United States was the woman known as Madame Alexander. Born in 1895, in Brooklyn, New York, Bertha Alexander (she later changed her name to Beatrice) was a major figure in the doll business from the time she founded the Alexander Doll Company in 1923 until her death at age 95 on October 3, 1990. Her success was due to her outlook on life. She was a woman ahead of her time, never settling for traditional roles. Rather, she believed she could be a businesswoman, and worked hard to be a successful one. The company, which she sold in 1988, still continues today,

producing quality dolls that are beloved by both children and collectors.

Madame Alexander's story starts in the nineteenth century, with the birth of her father, Maurice Alexander, in the Black Sea port of Odessa. Forced to leave Russia because of his political activities while a student, he went to Germany where he learned how to repair dolls, clocks, and china. In 1891 Maurice emigrated to the United States and was befriended by a New York City businessman who imported doll parts from Germany. With the help of the importer, he founded the Alexander Doll Hospital and store on Grand Street in New York City's Lower East Side.

It was in New York that Maurice met and married Hannah, an Austrian immigrant. The couple had four daughters, Beatrice being the oldest. Beatrice was a precocious and sometimes difficult child. In a 1988 interview with Krystyna Poray Goddu for *Dolls*, Madame told a story of slapping one of her father's customers. The Alexander family lived in an apartment above the doll hospital, which was frequented by the wealthy carriage trade. One evening, when Beatrice was about six, her mother woke her up because a wealthy client wanted to hold her. The woman played with Beatrice's long curls, stretching them out and letting them snap back. Beatrice, however, soon tired of this game, and slapped the woman!

Despite the fact that the family was in the doll business, or maybe because of it, Madame didn't play with dolls as a child. She was an avid reader in her youth and a diligent student. Education was important to her parents, and they passed this value to their daughter, who graduated from high school as the valedictorian of her class. She continued her education in business school.

In 1911, shortly before Beatrice completed her studies, the bank in which her parents had their money failed and they lost their savings. This event had a great impact on Madame, making her even more determined to become a financial success. At the age of seventeen she became a bookkeeper for Irving Hat Stores. At this point she was making more money than her fiancé, Phillip Berhman, who worked at a local hat factory.

During World War I Maurice Alexander wasn't able to import the German dolls that were a mainstay of his business, thus opening the way for Madame's entry into the dollmaking business. The first "Madame Alexander" dolls, created with the help of her three sisters, were Red Cross Nurses made of cloth, and sold through her father's shop. The success of this family venture prompted Madame, despite the fact that she was the mother of eight-year-old Mildred (who, Madame admitted on many an occasion, was the greatest joy of her life), to found the Alexander Doll Company in 1923. To start, Madame obtained a loan for $1,600, which covered the rent on a place in downtown Manhattan, the cost of some furniture, and a sewing machine. She didn't have enough money for tools and dies, so the first official Alexander dolls were made of muslin.

The early years were hard for this pioneering woman. She found a friend to watch Mildred while she worked, sometimes until midnight. Then, she recalled in a 1988 interview, "After a day's work, I cleaned, I cooked. I worked hard. I had my ideals. I made a big sacrifice; I gave up many things I would have enjoyed." It was difficult being a woman in an arena dominated by men. Her solution, she said, was to always behave like a lady in her role as businessperson. In a 1984 interview with doll expert John Axe, Madame said, "This put me at a disadvantage with my competitors in the early years, but I believe it has paid off in the end." It was her distinctive ladylike way of doing business that earned her the nickname "Madame."

In the early years, Madame ran the Alexander Doll Company by herself while her husband Phillip kept his job in the hat industry. Eventually it became apparent that help was needed in managing the business. Confident in her ultimate success, Madame asked her husband to join the company. Afraid the family wouldn't be able

A ten-inch hard-plastic Southern Belle by Madame Alexander, circa 1971-73

to live on the income from her business, Phillip was hesitant. Madame was determined that nothing would get in the way of her dream, and persisted in needling her husband until she wore down his resistance. Phillip remained an essential part of the Alexander Doll Company until his death in 1969.

The earliest Alexander dolls were of cloth and wore attractive outfits of the highest quality. The Alexander dolls' clothing has always been known for the elaborate attention given to detail in its design and execution. For four years in a row, from 1951 to 1954, Madame won the Fashion Academy's gold medal for her dolls' clothing. In the 1930s the company began producing composition dolls, and it was the composition Dionne Quints, released in 1935, that made Madame Alexander a household name. In 1937 Alexander introduced another runaway hit, its Scarlett O'Hara doll. It is one of the company's most lasting series, as a version of Scarlett has been in the line almost continuously since its introduction. (The Little Women series is the longest running, first made in cloth in 1933.) The company switched to hard plastic in 1948. Popular dolls made in this medium are the Alexanderkins, introduced in 1953; Cissy, introduced in 1955; and Cissette, introduced in 1957.

In the 1950s Madame moved her operation to a factory in Harlem, where it remains today. Over the years, the Alexander Doll Company has produced more than 5,000 different doll models at the factory. In 1988 Madame sold the company to Jeff Chodorow and Ira Smith. They continue to manufacture the famed Alexander dolls, which are still renowned for their quality clothing, now designed by Therese Stadelmeier and Daun Fallon. In addition to these dolls, the company manufactures dolls designed by German artist Hildegard Günzel and the Let's Play Dolls line designed by Robin Woods. In 1992, along with Stanley and Irene Wahlberg, the Alexander Doll Company purchased Effanbee, another old, established American company.

In looking over her accomplishments, Madame Alexander said in 1988, "I brought the industry of dollmaking

27

to this country after the war, when Germany had other things to do in their factories and made no dolls. We were starving here for dolls." In an era when most women stayed at home and raised families, Madame Alexander chose to pursue her dream and established an endearing tradition in the United States.

COLLECTING

As long as there have been things to collect, there have been collectors. Today, such diverse objects as figurines, prints, glassware, baseball cards, and matchbooks are collected. Among the most popular collectibles, along with stamps and coins, are dolls. In the United States the idea of collecting became popular with the growth of leisure time in the 1920s. Hobbies were encouraged as an educational pastime, and by the 1930s hobby shows were being held across the country. It was around this time that doll collectors began to get together to share their love of dolls and knowledge about them. Although there probably were individual doll collectors all over the United States, the doll clubs sprang up mainly in Eastern cities.

The Doll Collectors of America, Inc., founded on November 14, 1935, in Massachusetts, is believed to be the first incorporated doll club. Its objective, which was generally the objective of most doll collectors of that era, was the in-depth study of dolls past and present. The organization exhibited at the Chicago Antiques Exposition and Hobby Show and at the New York World's Fair in 1939. These exhibitions sparked the formation of many other doll clubs.

In 1937 the Women's Exposition of Arts and Industries invited a well-known New York City doll collector to gather some dolls for an exhibition. Not only did sixteen women volunteer to lend 500 dolls, but they also formed the National Doll and Toy Collectors Club (still in existence in New York City today). Because the charter members of this club came from all over the North-

east, club chapters soon appeared in cities other than New York. Within a few years there were chapters in every region of the United States.

Early collectors focused on the study of late eighteenth- and early nineteenth-century woodens, waxes, and papier-mâchés. The French and German bisques, so popular today, weren't of major interest then, mainly because they were still being produced. Over time, more and more collectors became interested in the French porcelain fashionable lady dolls and the bébés of Jumeau and Bru, but the German bisques were given little consideration until much later. Most early collectors played with them as children and thought of them as toys. It was not uncommon to find these dolls in thrift shops, junk stores, and even in the garbage!

By the 1940s there was more organization to the doll-collecting movement as more clubs formed across the country. Part of this phenomenon can be attributed to World War II when few new dolls were being made, so interest in the antiques grew accordingly. In 1941 Janet Johl's *The Fascinating Story of Dolls*, the first book dedicated to the subject, was published. Johl said she wrote the book for "those interested in dolls, from the children who play with them, love and cherish them, to the collector who prizes them, and the student who enjoys them for the research they afford in educational and ethnological fields." Although there were no magazines dedicated exclusively to dolls at that time, *Hobbies* had been including information on dolls in every issue, and had even established a "Dollology" department.

Eleanor St. George, in her late 1940s doll classic, *The Dolls of Yesterday*, stated, "Except for the tulip craze in Holland, it is doubtful if any hobby has ever grown more rapidly than this one," and it certainly seems that way. As the 1950s rolled around, doll collecting just seemed to blossom. The United Federation of Doll Clubs (UFDC), a national group providing organization and guidelines for doll clubs around the United States, was formed in 1949 and held its first national convention in September 1950 in New London, Connecticut. Forty-four years later this organization boasts a membership of 600 clubs, including some 15,000 collectors worldwide.

Although antiques were the most popularly collected dolls, some collectors were interested in what were then contemporary manufactured works, such as the composition Patsy, Dy-Dee, and Magic Skin Baby, all of which are highly collectible today. Contemporary artist-made dolls, which are those most popular with collectors now and that make up the bulk illustrated in this book, were not in abundance. The National Doll and Toy Collectors Club was one of the few organizations that encouraged the small number of people making dolls at that time. Handmade dolls were always included in its exhibitions and competitions, and Dorothy Heizer, Muriel Bruyere, and Gertrude Florian, three of the top early artists, were among its members.

The UFDC's efforts to educate collectors resulted in a growing appreciation and enthusiasm for original artist dolls. In 1963 UFDC member Helen Bullard founded the National Institute of American Doll Artists (NIADA) to promote interest in, and appreciation of, original dolls. This organization started with eleven artist-members and now has more than fifty. NIADA artists have always been considered the top of the field.

Despite the efforts of NIADA and other artists' groups, collectors' interests through the 1970s still focused on antiques. Of course, as more and more collectors began buying antique dolls, the prices for them rose and by the late 1970s they had soared far beyond the pace of inflation. This boom has continued until today; for example, on August 8, 1993, a rare 1884 bisque exhibition Jumeau sold for $231,000 (with buyer's premium) at a Frasher's Doll Auction sale setting a record. This was then broken on February 8, 1994, when a 1909 Kämmer & Reinhardt bisque sold for $282,825 at Sotheby's, London. The boom has been attributed to the formation of auction houses specializing in dolls, the increase in the number of doll dealers and in the professionalism of their business practices, and in the increased publicity for dolls, particularly with the apprearance of magazines devoted exclu-

sively to dolls, such as *Dolls: The Collector's Magazine* that published its first issue in 1982.

Soon the average collector couldn't afford more than one or two antiques, if any, and that led to the growth of what's known as reproduction dolls—new dolls made from molds taken from antiques. These dolls are made with the same materials as the antiques and are painted, wigged, and dressed in the same manner as the originals. They are virtually identical to the antiques except in price: reproductions are affordable.

Artist Dolls

By the early 1980s a new face was appearing in the doll world. American dollmakers were moving away from making reproductions of antiques to creating their own originals. Tired of painstakingly copying the work of what were really mass-produced pieces once intended as toys, the artists wanted to use their talents to develop their own creations. Artists' originals of the early 1980s, which were almost without exception made of porcelain, tended to depict young girls. Although their faces had more character than a bébé, the features were mostly idealized and expressionless. They were unquestionably dolls, nearly always dressed in pretty, vintage-style clothes.

At about the same time the doll artist movement started in Germany. Probably because of the country's long dollmaking tradition, this art form continued to be practiced in West Germany after World War II, despite the lack of commercial production. The reproduction movement was quite strong, and many classes were taught throughout the country. However, unlike in the United States, there were just small pockets of people making dolls, and for the most part, they had no contact with each other.

In 1982 the Global Doll Society (GDS) held its annual convention in Frankfurt, and American artist Astry Campbell gave a lecture on American artist dolls. Captivated by the creations they saw, the German artists began producing their own work. The following year the GDS convention in Limburg and Frankfurt held its first competition for artist dolls. There were so many entries that the results took much longer to be calculated than anticipated, and entrants who waited for the results missed their trains home. By the mid-1980s German artists, including Brigitte Deval, Sabine Esche, Hildegard Gunzel, Annette Himstedt, and Rotraut Schrott, were creating stunningly realistic dolls sculpted directly from resin-based oven-cured modeling materials such as Fimo, Sculpey, and Cernit.

In 1985 many of the works of these German artists were published in *Kunstler Puppen* (Art Dolls) by Joachim F. Richter. When this book appeared in the United States it had tremendous impact on American doll artists, who began creating their own realistic works that ranged from dimpled crying babies to wrinkled old women. This movement toward realism in dolls continues today, and it seems that each year the quality of dolls created by artists around the world gets better and better.

By comparison, the doll movement in France is just beginning to get started. The French were relative latecomers to the antique collecting field and even later to the contemporary artist domain. In the early 1980s the French were still primarily collecting antiques, disdaining the celluloid, felt, and plastic works from the early twentieth century; few were collecting contemporary pieces. While in America, Germany, and even Great Britain, the doll artist movement was gaining full speed by the mid-1980s, it was just starting to make a mark in France, due to the efforts of a small number of artisans scattered over the country. Although there is no official artists' association, the biannual arts and crafts fair in Paris, the Salon des Ateliers d'Art et de Création, has featured dolls at each event. According to Barbara Spadaccini-Day of the Musée des Arts Décoratifs in Paris, a growing appreciation for modern artist dolls seems to be developing.

All dolls, whether designed for play or for adult collectors, begin with an artist. In some cases the artist simply provides illustrations showing how he or she wants the doll to look; a second artist then sculpts the head and, perhaps, the limbs and body for the doll based on these illustrations. In the world of collectible dolls, however, the artist who conceives the idea for the doll is usually its sculptor, whether the doll is a one-of-a-kind creation, part of a limited edition, or mass-produced. But sculpting is not the only skill needed to make a doll. A doll must also be painted and dressed. Hence a doll artist is also a painter, costume designer, and often a pattern maker and expert seamstress. Some doll artists are also mold makers, wig makers, hairstylists, and shoemakers. No other art form demands the multitude of skills that are necessary in the making of a doll.

How much work an artist does on a doll varies, of course. If a doll is manufactured by a company in large numbers, the artist has probably sculpted, as well as painted and costumed, a prototype for production. The manufacturer then creates molds from the prototype and mass-produces the doll, generally in porcelain or vinyl. If the doll is a limited edition, the artist is often more involved. How much work he or she personally does generally decreases as the edition size increases. For example, if a doll is being issued in an edition of, say, 500 or 1,000, the doll is probably being produced in a factory. The artist has done the original sculpture, designed the original costume, and supplied patterns for all clothing items. He or she may supervise the production of the doll and, perhaps, do some of the painting. If, however, the doll is being issued in an edition of fifty, the artist could be doing all the sculpting and painting, but may have helpers pouring the porcelain slip into the molds, removing the doll from the molds, cleaning and firing it, and cutting and sewing the costumes, as well as assembling and dressing the dolls. (Because of the cost of the rotational molds used to make vinyl dolls, they are rarely limited to editions of less than 250 pieces.) If that same doll is issued in a very small edition, such as five or ten pieces, the artist is almost always doing all the work on the dolls in his or her own studio, including making all the clothing and accessories. If the doll is a one-of-a-kind, it's safe to assume all the work on it has been done personally by the artist.

Today's collectible dolls are available in a wide price range—from under a hundred dollars to many thousands. A variety of factors determine the price, including the number of dolls made from the original sculpture (i.e., the size of the edition) and how much work the original artist has done on the doll. Obviously, if a doll is manufactured in large quantities, its price would be less than for a one-of-a-kind creation, just as the price for a print is less than that of an original oil painting. The reputation of the artist also plays a role in pricing, as does the quality of the doll and the materials used for its costume. Many of today's one-of-a-kind dolls and those issued in small editions are garbed in costumes made from antique fabrics and have accessories that may include precious or semiprecious stones. The time the artist spends in searching for antique silks, brocades, and lace, and the money he or she spends on them and on accessories, must be factored into the asking price for the doll. What's surprising, though, is that there are beautiful dolls available in such a wide price range. One reason for this is that many of the companies selling collectible dolls today are utilizing the talents of top artists—artists who make only one-of-a-kind dolls or dolls in very small editions—to create original sculptures for dolls that the company then reproduces in large numbers.

Collectible dolls are sold in several ways. Many collectors have been introduced to art dolls—dolls designed for adults—via the home-shopping networks on television. Also, there are a number of companies that sell dolls by mail, such as the Ashton-Drake Galleries, Franklin Mint, Danbury Mint, Georgetown Collection, and the Hamilton Collection. Through extensive advertising and mass mailings, companies such as these have contributed greatly to the acceptance of dolls as collectible works of art. There are also thousands of stores worldwide that specialize in collectible dolls. In order to compete with television selling and the mail-order houses, the owners of these stores are generally service oriented. Most owners of doll stores are very well-informed about the dolls they carry and the artists who made them, and they'll willingly share this knowledge with customers. Many also host guest appearances by artists where the customers get a chance to meet informally with the artist and have the artist sign their dolls.

Doll collecting seems to be a continually growing field, both in the number of people who enjoy it and in the types of dolls created. For those of you who are new to the doll world, we hope the glimpse we've offered into this exciting hobby has whetted your appetite for more.

The World's
MOST BEAUTIFUL
Dolls

This German-born artist, who's lived in Italy since 1974, has been creating dolls since she was a child. Her first adult-made creations were carved wood puppet sets, which she began working on in 1959 after being inspired by the dolls, puppets, marionettes, and crèche figures she found in Munich's museums. It wasn't until 1968 that Brigitte Deval made the first of the wax-over-ceramic dolls for which she's known today.

Deval does create some one-of-a-kinds; however, most of her pieces, like the *Girl with Puppet* crafted in 1981, are done in small limited editions. Yet each doll in an edition is unique in some small way. "All the pieces are different," the dollmaker explains. "I open the mouth a little differently or change the expression a bit. I normally work so free and do whatever I am feeling." To watch this artist at work, which is easy to do as she often can be found completing her dolls during the many personal appearances she makes throughout the year, is to see an artist who is truly at one with her creation.

Deval is very versatile; the dolls she's created represent the spectrum of humankind. The only thing they all have in common is the intense expression on their faces, an expression the artist tries to achieve so that her dolls look like they "have a brain." Deval's work is made of only the finest materials. The glass eyes are made by a Roman craftsman who makes glass eyes for humans; the silk fabrics used for the costumes are woven to Deval's specifications in Florence; the stockings are knit in Romania, and the wigs are made from mohair or human hair in Germany.

Universally regarded as one of the top doll artists in the world, Brigitte Deval can command thousands of dollars for her work. However, she has also done some designs for The Ashton-Drake Galleries of Niles, Illinois, and the Georgetown Collection of Portland, Maine, so there are Brigitte Deval designs that are more affordable to collectors.

Brigitte Starczewski Deval, *Girl with Puppet*

This South Carolina artist's thirty-inch porcelain *Goldilocks* is accompanied by a sweet baby bear wearing a felt vest trimmed with pinecones, whose chair she's just broken. Created in 1994, the fairy-tale sweetheart has blond curled hair topped off with a rose velvet hat and blue blown-glass eyes. Her cloth body contains a skeleton, allowing her to be positioned in many ways. The white flower-trimmed blouse and blue print dress are cotton.

Storybook characters are a favorite of Resch's, whose porcelain dolls mainly depict children and fashion ladies. She also does portrait dolls and says that many of her family members have been her subjects. "I am always looking for appealing faces," she says, "with a certain sweetness and innocence." All her porcelain dolls are done in small editions of twenty or twenty-five pieces because Resch does everything herself. The only help she has is from her daughter, who sews some of the clothing, all made from natural fabrics such as cotton and silk.

Born and raised in Pennsylvania, Resch has always made dolls in some form, whether they were soap dolls for her childhood dollhouse or apple-head dolls later on. She created her first porcelain doll in 1978 and has won many awards for her work since then. In addition to her porcelains her Murrells Inlet, South Carolina, company, Original Dolls and Molds by Thelma Resch, produces some vinyl pieces and molds for hobbyists.

Thelma Resch, *Goldilocks*

nna Avigail Brahms is, more than any other doll art-
ist, *the* pioneer in the field of the contemporary artist doll. She
began crafting dolls in 1976, but she didn't become known until
1980, when Thomas Boland, an artists' representative, who went
on to manage many of today's other top dollmakers, agreed to act
as her agent. American collectors, who were just starting to ap-
preciate the concept of an "artist doll," were then treated to one-
of-a-kind Fimo creations that were more realistic than anything
they had ever seen. And dozens of artists, upon seeing Brahms'
work for the first time, were inspired to make more realistic dolls,
dolls that resembled art more than playthings, beginning a trend
that continues to this day. Since those early years her work has
been exhibited in the windows of Saks Fifth Avenue and Tiffany's,
the Gallery of Performing Arts at Lincoln Center in New York
City, and the Musée des Arts Décoratif at the Louvre in Paris.

Her dolls are one-of-a-kinds made of Fimo, like the 1992 creation shown here. Their cotton bodies have a wire armature so
that the dolls can be posed; however, the Israeli-born dollmaker
explains, "I position the doll the way I want it to be. I can change
the posture, but I don't like other people to change it." Their hair
is of angora, and is dyed to Brahms' specifications by the woman
who raises the goats from which it comes. An Anna Avigail Brahms
doll starts at a few thousand dollars.

Anna Avigail Brahms, *Girl with Dark Hair*

The story of this world-renowned doll artist goes back twenty years to when Anna Avigail Brahms was living in Israel, and crafted a puppet of papier-mâché simply because, she says, "It just came to me." From there she went on to carving wood puppets and dolls for an ethnological exhibit of dolls for the Museum of Jerusalem. Soon she switched to Fimo, and with the sale of her first Fimo dolls she was able to pay for her family's move to France. The sale of her dolls supported them during the year they lived there. When she moved to the United States in 1980 her work was immediately picked up by Thomas Boland of Chicago, one of today's best-known doll representatives. He made Anna Avigail Brahms a household name among doll collectors.

Brahms begins each day with "a short period of meditation, just before I start to work. Sometimes," she explains, "while I am meditating I see exactly what I am going to do that day. I know the doll; I see details of the angle of the head, the eyes, what kind of person it is going to be." The twenty-three-inch-high, one-of-a-kind Fimo work shown here, which is untitled, as many of the artist's creations are, was visualized as a young girl who needed a doll to hold. She has inset blue glass eyes and an angora goat hair wig. She's dressed in a wonderful combination of a light-colored silk nightgown and black stockings.

Anna Avigail Brahms, *Untitled*

A native of Arizona now residing in Southern California. Julia Rueger was a certified ceramics teacher before she began creating dolls. She made her first original doll in 1986 and says, "Once I started making dolls, I never turned back. My love for dolls and interest in them just keeps growing, and I have a need to keep learning." Known for her portrayals of young children, such as *Cirby*, her dolls evoke the innocence and wonder of youth.

Rueger sculpts her originals in either clay or Plastilina. This sculpture is then used to make molds for porcelain dolls, which she creates in limited editions of ten to thirty-five pieces each. "All my dolls are handmade," says the artist. "I design all the costumes, choose the fabrics and accessories, and sculpt, clean, and paint every doll myself." In addition to creating her artist dolls, which are sold through her company, Julia Rueger, Ltd., of Crestline, California, she has designed dolls for the Hamilton Collection of Jacksonville, Florida.

Cirby is typical of the artist's work. Introduced in 1994, the twenty-seven-inch-high doll is from a limited edition of thirty-five. The doll has a porcelain head, arms, and legs on a cloth body with a wire armature. Her wig is made of lambskin, and she has inset blue-gray glass paperweight eyes. *Cirby* wears a blue crushed-velvet hat, a gardening smock with cropped blue pants, and leather shoes. She comes with a wheelbarrow and an eggplant.

Julia Rueger, *Cirby*

*I*n the true English tradition, the British dollmaking duo of Paul Crees and Peter Coe create their dolls of poured wax. They have been experimenting with their medium of choice for years and have been quite innovative with it. They have developed a special matte finish that not only gives their work realistic flesh tones, but makes the wax flexible enough to allow the parts to bend and absorb shock, which considerably cuts down on the breakage of their pieces.

Crees made his first dolls in 1978 of plaster of paris and Styrofoam. They were done to look like Marlene Dietrich and dressed in outfits from her various film roles, as Crees collected the actress' memorabilia. A few years later, Crees and Coe began experimenting with wax. *Windswept Woman of Lyme*, in a limited edition of ten, is a prime example of the poured-wax dolls they are creating today. She stands twenty-eight inches high, as do all the dolls in the Paul Crees Collection, since the dollmakers feel that this size allows for accurately detailed costumes.

The elaborate clothing of the Crees and Coe dolls are another of their trademarks. *The Windswept Woman of Lyme* wears an elegant purple silk cloak over a gray, silver, and black day gown of Japanese silk jacquard trimmed with French cotton lace. Many of their dolls, however, wear much more ornate creations. It's no wonder, as both artists have a background in theater and costume design. They do all the work on the costumes and the dolls themselves, creating about 100 pieces a year. The Dorset-based artists are proud of their creations, particularly those done in wax. "It's nice," says Coe, "to feel we're still keeping alive a tradition of dollmaking that goes back to more than a century before the advent of bisque and porcelain doll manufacture."

Paul Crees and Peter Coe, *Windswept Woman of Lyme*

This French artist is admired worldwide for her realistic portrayals of contemporary youth. Her dolls are so realistic that when seen in photographs they are often mistaken for real children, and when seen "in person" the lifelike creations look uncanny because of their one- to two-foot height.

The Paris-born artist became involved with dolls after meeting doll artist Anna Avigail Brahms in the early 1980s. "I made some dresses for her dolls," says Mitrani, "and she showed me how to make a doll. That was the big start." Although her earliest works were influenced by Brahms, she wanted to create pieces from her own soul and spirit. She says she is fascinated by human beings, their expressions and feelings, and that shows in her work. "When I started to work," she says, "the doll world was still bound by the past, inspired by antique dolls with lace and old fabrics and the nostalgic atmosphere of things past. I loved it, and I still love it. But I was fascinated and moved by the children of today. I find them beautiful, with an infinite range of expressions." In 1985 the first of her "children of the twentieth century were born," she notes. Mitrani's trademark, as exhibited on the dolls shown on the following pages, is red hair and freckles.

The artist does not name her dolls, which are all one-of-a-kinds with heads and limbs sculpted of Fimo. They have mohair wigs and glass eyes. She makes only about twenty a year, and they are snatched up for sums that have gone as high as tens of thousands of dollars.

Anne Mitrani, *Untitled*

Anne Mitrani, *Untitled*

Anne Mitrani, *Untitled*

*T*his German-born artist is known for her porcelain and vinyl depictions of pensive little girls, which she's been making since the mid-1980s. Her company, Sonja Hartmann Originals, was founded in Berlin, but relocated to Glenmoore, Pennsylvania, in 1989. For a few years the artist traveled back and forth between her home in Germany and the United States, but in 1993 she and her family settled here.

Like so many dollmakers, Hartmann made her first doll for her young daughter. Made in the early 1980s, it was a stuffed cloth toy. A passion for creating propelled her forward, and soon she was sculpting with Fimo because, she explains, she wanted to achieve more expression. In 1983 Hartmann decided she wanted to make porcelain dolls, but this presented a challenge as she couldn't find anyone to teach her the basics. For help she called the Royal Porcelain manufactory of Berlin, and they invited her to spend a day at their operations. This was the extent of her training in the medium. In 1988 she successfully introduced her work in the United States, and it wasn't long after that the artist teamed up with an American businessman and moved her studio here.

Anja was introduced by Sonja Hartmann in 1992. Typical of the artist's work, the vinyl doll, which stands twenty-three inches high, has a ten-piece ball-jointed body. The face is hand painted by Hartmann, as is the face of every doll that bears the artist's name, which means she paints literally thousands a year. Although the trend for dollmakers seems to be toward creating dolls as sculptured works of art, Hartmann has no plans to head in that direction. "I want to keep a bit of the toy in my doll," says the artist. "I like to have that plaything idea behind my dolls."

Sonja Hartmann, *Anja*

*T*his little girl named *Medley* is little indeed. Just 6½ inches high, the all-porcelain doll is typical of the miniatures created by California artist Joanne Callander. "I love the feeling of being able to hold a tiny child, fully contained, in the palm of my hand. They look so precious and protected there," the artist says, adding, "the image symbolizes to me the precious and protected state all children could enjoy if we could live in an ideal world."

The artist sculpts her originals, which she has been making since 1982, in Fimo; she uses the sculptures to create the molds for her porcelain dolls. While she occasionally creates one-of-a-kinds, most of her dolls are issued in limited editions of ten to forty pieces. Although tiny, averaging just 5½ to 6½ inches high, Callander's porcelains are big on detail and personality. They have seven to nine joints, so they can be positioned in a variety of poses. They all have intricately detailed costumes, such as *Medley's* printed cotton jumpsuit, silk apron, and embroidered cotton jacket. Inset eyes of Fimo or resin are made by the artist, and wigs are handmade of rooted mohair or lamb's wool.

The self-taught artist, who made her first doll as a Christmas gift for a doll-collecting uncle, leaves the interpretation of her work to the viewer. "Not everyone can create with their hands; that's the artist's job," Callander notes. "But everyone can create with their heads and their hearts. I hope those who see my work are inspired to look within themselves and find elements of their own personality or an 'inner playful spirit' to bestow on my dolls."

Joanne Callander, *Medley*

*T*he daughter of artists, Virginia Ehrlich Turner purposely avoided arts and crafts in her youth because, she says, "I always thought my life would have been less hectic if my parents hadn't been artists." Despite this, in the 1980s she began making porcelain reproductions and soon, she explains, "what was a hobby developed into a business." In 1989, after taking some sculpting seminars, she created her first original doll. Today the artist prefers to work with Plastiline or clay and bases many of her pieces on actual children. Her Turner Dolls, Inc., of Heltonville, Indiana, produces the artist's limited-edition porcelains; edition sizes range from 50 to 500 pieces. Turner Dolls has a reputation for quality work, from the cleaning of the porcelain, which gives the dolls their smooth, flawless complexions, to the pristine painting of their features. In addition to the work she does with her own company, the artist has designed dolls for the Hamilton Collection.

Turner is best known for her large-size, realistic-looking babies and toddlers, such as her 1992 *Baby Joe Michael*, seen here with three different hair colors, and 1991 *Kitty Kay*. Most of the artist's dolls have porcelain heads, arms, and legs on soft bodies with wire armatures. Twenty-one-inch *Baby Joe Michael* and *Kitty Kay* have porcelain heads and hands, but their arms and legs, as well as their bodies, are cloth. Unlike the majority of her dolls, these are filled with pellets, which give them the feel and weight of a real child, and allows one to position them in a variety of poses.

Virginia Ehrlich Turner, *Baby Joe Michael* **and** *Kitty Kay*

Born in northern Germany, Hanna Kahl-Hyland began drawing and painting portraits of fairy-tale characters during her youth. Her mother, a gifted artist and musician, recognized and encouraged her daughter's talent, arranging for her to have lessons in painting and sculpting during her early years. After marriage and a move to England, the artist studied sculpting at St. Martin's School of Arts in London. Twenty years ago she and her husband moved to the United States; they now reside in Connecticut. Kahl-Hyland created wood and stone sculptures until the early 1980s when, she says, "I became aware of contemporary dolls as an exciting art form. The creation of dolls enables me to use many of my artistic skills, such as sculpting, woodcarving, painting, and fashion designing. My interest and enjoyment in the creation of dolls has now become a passion."

Kahl-Hyland creates her one-of-a-kind dolls in wood and Paper-clay and does all the work on them herself. Because of the length of time each doll takes, she makes only a few a year. Some of her creations are translated into porcelain by Seymour Mann, Inc., of New York City. She is best known for her serene and beautiful fashion dolls and fairy-tale characters, such as *Cinderella*. This twenty-two-inch-high, one-of-a-kind doll has a basswood head over which several layers of oil paint have been applied; its body and limbs are a combination of wood, wire, and cloth. Her *Cinderella* has a mohair wig and painted eyes and is jointed at the shoulders, elbows, hips, and knees. She wears an antique French lace and satin dress and has a hand-beaded glass slipper.

Hanna Kahl-Hyland, *Cinderella*

The extraordinary dolls of Joelle Lemasson, who is known internationally as Héloïse, are on permanent display in a number of Swiss and French museums, including the Musée des Arts Décoratif at the Louvre. The Nantes artist made her first original doll in 1976. It was fashioned of fabric, as were her other early works. But she discovered resin in 1982 and has worked with it ever since, as she feels it best captures the translucent complexion of a child. Héloïse's dolls have an ethereal beauty that evokes forgotten memories of childhood and, according to the artist, "can be defined as both modern and romantic; childlike, but not childish."

Héloïse's dolls begin as clay sculptures, which are used to make molds for the resin pieces. Once the dolls are removed from the molds, the artist uses additional resin to define the features and to give each individual piece its own personality. She does the majority of the work on her dolls, including designing all their clothing. "I like to use fine silk taffetas, Swiss cotton, handmade embroideries, antique laces, and antique fabrics for their outfits," she says.

The artist has been creating one-of-a-kind dolls since 1993. Most of her dolls, however, are created in limited editions, ranging in size from just eight pieces up to one hundred. *La Grâce* is limited to an edition of eight; however, each of the eight dolls wears a one-of-a-kind dress. The twenty-four-inch, all-resin doll is costumed in antique lace and has a mohair wig and blue painted eyes. *La Grâce* is jointed at the hips only and, says the artist, "is my first doll made like a sculpture."

Héloïse, *La Grâce*

Wendy Lawton's dolls—produced by the Lawton Doll Company of Turlock, California, in limited editions of 50 to 750 pieces—are crisp, realistic portraits of children. The artist, who majored in home economics and minored in art at California's San Jose State University, says that dollmaking "was a natural outgrowth of my lifelong love of dolls, and the perfect expression for my training in art and textiles." Since Lawton created her first original doll in 1979, she has sculpted well over one hundred faces. "Each new face defines the child in a new way," she says, adding, "our faces are, perhaps, the key to our dolls." While there is no doubt that the faces of Lawton's dolls are captivating, the artist's talent as a clothing designer is obvious in the charming and imaginative outfits worn by her dolls. Also noteworthy are the delightful accessories that accompany many of her porcelain children.

The California artist has an extensive collection of children's books, and many of her works are inspired by children's stories and poems. Others depict customs of different cultures or are based on historical characters, such as *The Dreamer*, a 1994 doll from Lawton's Treasured Tales collection. This all-porcelain depiction of Joseph in his coat of many colors is fourteen inches high. Under his coat, which is lined in gold, is a gauze tunic; on his feet are laced-up sandals. *The Dreamer* has a synthetic-fiber wig and inset, brown acrylic eyes; it is jointed at the neck, shoulders, and hips.

Wendy Lawton, *The Dreamer*

Catherine Refabert became involved with dolls in 1960 when she married Jacques Refabert, whose family owned the Clodrey doll company. Now the designer for Corolle, a company in Langeais, France, that she and her husband founded in 1979, she creates baby play dolls and fashion dolls. These are mass-produced in vinyl and distributed worldwide. "Corolle's philosophy is to offer children the very best," says Refabert. "A Corolle doll is fabulous for a little girl to play with and love, and it is very fashionable for an adult, too," she says. "That is our secret."

Refabert's fashion dolls are dressed in the French fashions of today, as in the case of *Danielle*, or of the past, like *Charlotte*, that has a 1930s-style outfit. Their clothing is made of the best French fabrics—pure cotton, chintz, or silk—done in prints created exclusively for Refabert. She says, "Corolle brings to collectors what France is known for: fashion and fabulous fabrics." *Danielle* was produced in 1992 in a limited edition of 150 pieces worldwide; she is the only Corolle doll produced in such a small quantity. Generally, edition sizes range from 500 to 1,500.

The babies and children in the *Cousin-Cousine Family* of dolls are "designed to be hugged and loved," as are all the play dolls designed by Refabert. "Once a little girl made a drawing of a doll for me," says the artist when describing how these works originated, "and asked me to turn it into a doll. That is the story behind *Cousin-Cousine*: a little boy and a little girl that live in children's drawings and dreams."

Catherine Refabert, *Danielle*

Catherine Refabert, *Cousin-Cousine Family*

Catherine Refabert, *Charlotte*

*J*an McLean, New Zealand's best-known doll artist, comes from a talented family. Her great-uncle, Gordon McIntyre, was a well-known cartoonist; her maternal grandmother sculpted; and for a short time, her mother worked as a portrait artist. As a child McLean enjoyed sketching, and after marriage she made pottery as a hobby. But her professional training was in nursing, and she worked as a nurse for more than twenty years before making her first doll.

In 1983 while working on her family genealogy McLean decided to make a doll for her daughter, she says, "because my grandmother had made one for me." She enrolled in a dollmaking course and made several porcelain reproductions. A few years later German doll artist Hildegard Günzel visited New Zealand with Mathias Wanke, a show organizer who also owned a company that sold molds and other dollmaking supplies. It was meeting Günzel and seeing her artist dolls that inspired McLean to create her own originals; she completed her first in 1987.

Because of the isolation of New Zealand, few people were aware of McLean's work until she exhibited her dolls at the 1991 American International Toy Fair in New York City. Dealers at this trade show went wild over her creations, and McLean went home with more orders than she could fill in a year. You can understand the excitement McLean caused when you look at *Pansy*, one of the pieces she showed at that 1991 event. This stunning twenty-eight-inch-high doll, limited to an edition of 100, has a porcelain head, arms, and legs on a cloth body. *Pansy* has a synthetic wig and inset blue paperweight eyes and comes with her rocking chair.

Jan McLean, *Pansy*

Jan McLean is best known for her large, twenty-eight- to fifty-inch-high porcelain dolls of little girls and adolescents. Some of her creations, like *Pansy*, have a feisty expression; others, like *Primrose*, are more wistful looking. All, however, have very realistic appearances, are exquisitely painted and costumed, and are perfectly proportioned (a result, no doubt, of the artist's training in anatomy and years spent as a nurse). McLean, who now heads her own company, Jan McLean Originals of Dunedin, New Zealand, creates both one-of-a-kinds and limited-edition porcelains; edition sizes range from 15 to 100 pieces. The artist sculpts her originals in clay and personally paints all her dolls, and oversees all stages of production.

Everything on a McLean doll is handmade, including the dolls' wigs, shoes, hats, and jewelry. And, says the artist, "All my dolls have 'extras,' such as a companion doll, a chair, or a specially designed stand." *Primrose*, for example, comes with a wooden rocking chair and holds a posy of dried flowers. Created in 1992 in an edition of one hundred, the thirty-four-inch-high doll is from the artist's Flowers of the Heart collection. *Primrose* has a porcelain head and limbs on a cloth body, a synthetic wig, and inset gray paperweight eyes. The doll is costumed in a lavender cotton dress trimmed with peach ribbons, a hand-knit French angora sweater, and peach leather pumps.

Jan McLean, *Primrose*

*B*orn in Frankfurt, Rotraut Schrott has been making original dolls since 1980. She credits her father, the well-known German artist Ludwig Adam, with teaching her how to paint and sculpt. He constantly stressed how important it is for an artist to understand anatomy and proportion. Because of this, Schrott says, "I take as much care in making my dolls' arms and legs as I do with sculpting their facial features." As a result, her dolls' wrists and ankles have natural-looking crease marks, her babies have little half-clenched fists, while many of her older children have hands sculpted to hold objects such as a stuffed animal or a curl of their hair. All their hands and feet have tiny, sculpted nails.

Of course, she does not neglect her dolls' faces. Their eyes, for instance, are sculpted of Cernit, then painted by the artist and covered with Cernit eyelids. Hand-tied human-hair eyelashes are inserted into the Cernit, and another layer of the sculpting medium is applied over the lid. Mouths also get great attention, as Schrott believes that the mouth is the most expressive facial feature. Some of her dolls have bright smiles and pearly-white teeth; others have shy smiles or mouths turned down in a pout. All appear very natural and hauntingly realistic.

Typical of the artist's work is this thirty-five-inch-high, one-of-a-kind doll. The doll's head, shoulder plate, lower arms, and legs are Cernit; the body and upper arms are cloth. His wig is made of natural European hair, and he has dark-brown painted eyes. He wears a knitted cap and a Peruvian-style outfit.

Rotraut Schrott, *Mario, Peruvian Boy*

*R*otraut Schrott is known worldwide for her international children as well as her portrait dolls of real children, such as *Sophia*. This thirty-inch-high, one-of-a-kind doll has a Cernit head, shoulder plate, lower arms, and legs; the doll's upper arms and body are cloth. She has a natural, European-hair wig and brown painted eyes. The doll's costume is an adaptation of a seventeenth-century style. The dress is made of old cotton fabric; the under-dress is made from embroidered white batiste. Tied around her head is an antique scarf decorated with roses.

Noted for their realism, Schrott's dolls have warm and tender expressions, although some of them, the artist says, "capture a moment of happiness, sadness, or even a roguish look." Her goal is to create dolls "the collector, for a short, wonderful moment, believes are alive, that they will try to speak with them or stroke them. I want to create dolls that appear to have a heart and soul."

Although the artist does not make her own wigs (they are created exclusively for her), all the other work on the dolls and their costumes is done solely by her, from scouring flea markets and antiques stores for the perfect fabrics and trims, to dressing the finished sculpture. Consequently, she creates fewer than a dozen new dolls annually and they sell for thousands of dollars. Some of her originals, however, are reproduced in porcelain and vinyl by the Great American Doll Company of Compton, California.

Rotraut Schrott, *Sophia*

*G*rowing up in Worcester, Massachusetts, Susan Wakeen and her twin sister loved playing with dolls, especially their Barbies. That was the extent of this artist's involvement with dolls until years later when she was working as a special education teacher in Boston. Unable to find a sculpting class in the area, Wakeen took a course in reproduction dollmaking. As is so often the case, she eventually began sculpting her own dolls and in 1985 she founded the Littlest Ballet Company.

"The most important feature of my dolls is the face," says Susan Wakeen. "I spend a lot of time making sure the sculpture is precise and honest in that it evokes a feeling inside me first. Each of my dolls has an attitude, such as curiosity, happiness, shyness, and that attitude or feeling is intentional." It's easy to see the innocence and wonder of the world in her *Amberley*. Big brown eyes peer out of her chubby face. This twenty-inch vinyl baby was introduced in 1990 by Wakeen's Canton, Connecticut–based firm, now called the Susan Wakeen Doll Company. She wears a dress of white diamond dobby trimmed with Venice lace. The large collar is accented with an appliqué.

Amberley is characteristic of the baby dolls Wakeen usually crafts, although the artist is also known for her ballerinas. Wakeen models her originals in Plasticine and then has them produced in vinyl, and occasionally porcelain, for her company. The dolls are limited to editions ranging from 500 to 2,500 pieces. She also works with the Danbury Mint of Norwalk, Connecticut, which translates her designs into porcelain.

Susan Wakeen, *Amberley*

*D*orothy Allison Hoskins was born in Texas, earned a bachelor of science degree in art education at Southern Illinois University, and then spent thirty years teaching art in Ohio elementary schools. It wasn't until she moved to Alaska, after falling in love with the state during a visit there, that she even thought about making dolls. One of her Alaskan friends crafted small-scale settings and, wanting to start some kind of business, Hoskins decided to create little people to populate those scenes. Hence, in 1984 the artist made her first original doll. All her early works were miniatures sculpted in Super Sculpey on a scale of one inch to the foot. Ranging from four to six inches in height, these dolls were very realistic and exquisitely detailed.

Hoskins soon became recognized for her exceptional work, and in 1990 she was invited to join the National Institute of American Doll Artists. Today she creates both Super Sculpey miniatures and larger, one-of-a-kind porcelain dolls. The artist has her own company, We Too, located in Fairbanks, and she has designed dolls for the Franklin Mint of Franklin Center, Pennsylvania.

Sleeping Beauties shows the artist's mastery of porcelain. The vignette features a 20½-inch woman with a porcelain head and limbs on a cloth body, a five-inch wax-over-porcelain baby, and a bed, also made by the artist. The woman has multiple joints, which allow her to be posed; the baby is all one piece.

Dorothy Allison Hoskins, *Sleeping Beauties*

Although Alaskan artist Dorothy Allison Hoskins initially earned recognition in the doll world for her dollhouse-scale miniatures, she is equally well known today for her beautiful porcelain creations, most of which depict adult women. In explaining these works the artist says, "They are sculpted directly in porcelain, so that means they are all one-of-a-kinds. I never make the same face twice. This keeps my work fresh. I don't create more than four to six dolls in a year, so I spend a lot of time thinking, revising, making them as perfect as possible. When they leave my hands, I want to know I've done the best that is in me to do. It's pure love."

Each of Hoskins' dolls is highly individualistic; however, all are elegant, graceful, optimistic. The woman in *To Life*, for example, is about to salute life with a toast; if there was hardship in her past, she's put it behind her and looks forward to the future. This 1993 creation is twenty inches high (11½ inches when seated). The doll artist used wax over porcelain for the head, arms, and legs, which gives it a luminous appearance; the body is cloth and wire. *To Life* is jointed at the shoulders, elbows, hips, and knees; the wig is constructed of mohair and the eyes are painted. The doll's dress is made of hand-embroidered antique cotton; the hat is of straw.

Dorothy Allison Hoskins, *To Life*

"I don't find inspiration in museums, and I don't have time to look at magazines. I collect pictures of children," says Munich-based Gaby Rademann. Even so, the artist says people are always telling her that her figures, including *Fritz*, a little shoe shine boy, look like her son. Whether *Fritz* has a family resemblance or not, this street urchin has the sweet, endearing look that is typical of Rademann's work. The doll is a thirty-one-inch-high, one-of-a-kind crafted in Cernit in 1991.

The dollmaker's first creation began with a porcelain blank, which she turned into a complete doll. This exercise, however, only whetted Rademann's appetite for more creation, and she soon began experimenting with Cernit. For years the only dolls available from this artist were one-of-a-kind creations in this medium. Then in the mid-1980s Rademann became friends with American artist Linda Mason, who eventually taught her how to make the molds for porcelain dolls. The only dolls Rademann now sells are porcelains done in editions of fifty to eighty pieces. All her dolls have mohair or human-hair wigs, human-hair eyelashes, and blown-glass eyes. The Ashton-Drake Galleries of Niles, Illinois mass-produces some of this artist's designs.

Gaby Rademann, *Fritz*

*S*usan Krey was born and raised in London and attended the Royal Society of Arts, majoring in fabric design. After finishing school she moved to Australia where she met and married Tim Krey, an American. Shortly after their 1967 marriage, the couple moved to Washington state, where they now reside in the town of Woodinville. Krey spent the next fifteen years raising a family; however, after the birth of her fifth child she felt the need to get back into art. She chose to make dolls, she says, "to express my artistic talent and be able to touch other people's hearts through a three-dimensional art form. I love children, and this is a way that I can express that love."

The artist made her first original doll in 1983 and hasn't stopped since. Her Krey Baby Doll Company is well known for the beauty of her porcelain children, such as *Summer*. This twenty-six-inch-high doll, made in 1993 in an edition of fifty, has a porcelain head, arms, and legs on a jointed cloth body.

Most of Susan Krey's porcelain dolls are issued in limited editions of twelve to one hundred pieces. However, vinyls of her designs are available from Dollmakers Originals International of Glenmoore, Pennsylvania, and the artist has designed dolls for The Ashton-Drake Galleries.

Susan Krey, *Summer*

*S*usan Krey is one of those dollmakers whom collectors catapulted into the limelight. She's soft spoken and modest, and the only criterion by which she judges her work is the impact it makes on her. "If a doll touches my heart, I think it might touch other people's, too," she says. Her thinking is obviously right on target, for ever since she created her first original doll in 1983 collectors have clamored for more.

The artist began exhibiting her dolls at shows near her Woodinville, Washington, home in the early 1980s and sold everything she made. When she ventured further afield, the same thing happened. Soon collectors across the United States were talking about her work, and the national press began taking notice of her artistry. Her dolls, most of which portray toddlers and young girls, are beautifully sculpted and painted, and wear charming contemporary outfits. Whether they bubble with the joy of childhood or have more pensive expressions, they exude a timeless quality that is captivating.

TJ, created by the artist in 1993, was featured on the cover of *Dolls'* November 1993 issue and is typical of Krey's realistic portrayals of young girls. This twenty-six-inch-high doll, limited to an edition of twenty-five pieces, has a porcelain head with sculpted teeth, porcelain limbs, and a cloth body. *TJ*'s wig is made of human hair; its inset eyes are light-blue blown glass.

Susan Krey, *TJ*

*M*onika Mechling, known to collectors simply as Monika (which is the name of her Arlington Heights, Illinois, company), began making dolls in 1979, she says, "to satisfy my creative desires, and combine my love of history, art, and femininity." She created elaborately costumed cloth figures until 1989, when she made her first original sculpted doll. Today she makes both one-of-a-kinds and limited-edition porcelain dolls; edition sizes range from ten to thirty-five. While she does all the work on her one-of-a-kinds, she does have some help with constructing the bodies and sewing the gowns for her limited-edition pieces.

"I believe deeply in the feminine desires of women, from gentle grace to passion itself," says the artist, who quickly gained wide recognition for her stunningly costumed and hauntingly beautiful porcelain ladies. *Lisabet* is typical of the artist's work. This nineteen-inch-high doll, issued in an edition of ten pieces, has a porcelain head, arms, and legs; its body is made of cloth and has a wire armature for poseability. The doll has a mohair wig and brown painted eyes; her gown and cloak, made of silk and silk chiffon, were inspired by the Art Nouveau period.

"To me the entire doll is important. The face, the pose, the costume, the movement of the hands, all combine to tell a story or evoke an emotion. These ladies have been stopped in mid-motion," she says, adding, "To know the emotions my dolls evoke is to know me."

Monika, *Lisabet*

*C*hristine Heath Orange began making rag dolls for her two daughters two decades ago. "This provided great enjoyment," she notes, "especially as we also made their clothes together." Her interest in dollmaking continued beyond her daughters' childhood though, and by 1990 she was creating original porcelains. The artist now has her own company, Christine Heath Orange Dolls of West Malvern, Worcester, but other than having help with sewing the dolls' clothes, does all the work on her originals herself. In addition to creating one-of-a-kinds and limited editions of ten to twenty-five pieces, Heath Orange has designed dolls for the Hamilton Collection.

The artist has already established an international reputation for her touching portrayals of children and their many moods. "Some are thoughtful, some happy, some anxious, or even a little sulky," says the artist. "Whatever the emotion is, the dolls must look as if they have thoughts and feelings, a soul." *Bryony* is an example of her pensive porcelain children. One of the artist's most popular 1992 creations, this twenty-three-inch doll was issued in an edition of twenty. "I have sculpted *Bryony* to sit in an unusual pose," notes Heath Orange, "with one leg tucked beneath her, leaning on one hand and clasping the baby doll in the other." *Bryony* wears a silk dress, petticoat, and pants; her porcelain baby doll is dressed in a matching outfit. "I enjoy using rich, expensive fabrics for clothing, and silks are a particular favorite," Heath Orange says. "All my dolls are in contemporary dress, all have human-hair wigs that I dye and style myself, and all have inset soft-glass eyes." Many also have accessories, such as a little doll, teddy bear, or book.

Christine Heath Orange, *Bryony*

*S*hortly after Hildegard Günzel sculpted her first doll in 1972, she began teaching dollmaking classes in her area of Germany. For years she continued to teach her sculpting method all over the world, and many of today's doll artists have received instruction and encouragement from this talented artist. Although she taught herself how to sculpt a doll, she learned how to work in porcelain from Mathias Wanke of M. Wanke GmbH, who offered classes in making reproductions of antiques. And it was Günzel's association with Wanke that eventually catapulted her into the international spotlight. First, in the early 1980s, Wanke made molds of the artist's original works, which were sold all over the world. Then, in the wake of this well-received venture, Wanke sent Günzel to the American International Toy Fair in New York City in 1986, where she became an overnight success.

Günzel's work depicts people of all ages, but she likes making girls and fairy-tale figures the best. Her dolls wear dreamy expressions and romantic-styled clothing. Their eyes are of mouth-blown German glass and their handmade wigs are of human hair or mohair. She has also begun creating porcelain busts, such as the two shown here, as they are much less time-consuming than the dolls.

Hildegard Günzel, *Two Busts*

*T*n the early 1970s Hildegard Günzel saw an antique doll collection at a friend's house. "This was the first collection of dolls I saw in my whole life," she recalls. "Before this I had no idea about collecting dolls." This eye-opening experience inspired the artist to begin making dolls. Prior to her involvement in dollmaking Günzel was a fashion designer, but after making her first doll she never wanted to go back to fashion. "When I modeled for the first time," she recalls, "I turned the head and touched it; I was able to touch it from all sides. This was a spectacular thing. It was totally different from what I had been doing, and once I started I never gave up."

Now she creates wax-over-porcelain one-of-a-kinds and limited editions for her own company, Studio Hildegard Günzel located in Duisburg, Germany. Two of her 1994 creations, thirty-six-inch *Sylvia* and thirty-two-inch *Melanie*, are shown here. They have mouth-blown German glass eyes and human-hair wigs. These works, done in limited editions of fifty each, sell for thousands of dollars from Günzel's German company. However, since 1990 the artist has been designing dolls for the Alexander Doll Company of New York City. The vinyl creations they manufacture are done in larger editions and sell at more affordable prices.

The artist has recently opened the first artist doll museum in Europe.

Hildegard Günzel, *Sylvia* and *Melanie*

*I*lse Wippler was born in Schwäbisch Gmünd and began drawing and modeling as a child. She has always loved dolls, and collected and restored antiques before creating her first original model in 1985. Today she creates one-of-a-kinds and porcelain dolls in limited editions of ten pieces at her Ilse Wippler - Restauration alter Puppen, located in Marktredwitz. Since 1990 the artist has also designed dolls for Sigikid, H. Scharrer & Koch GmbH, the internationally known German company located in Mistelbach, which issues her designs in vinyl. Wippler's Sigikid dolls are limited to editions of 500.

The artist is best known for her character dolls, which depict boys and girls from infants to teenagers. "Each model is made larger than life in Plasticine after a photograph of a child," says Wippler. "This sculpture is then turned into a doll upon reworking and shape reduction. Heads, breastplates, arms, and legs are modeled by myself and match the personality and size of the doll," she adds. It is the expression of a child in a photograph that captures Wippler's attention and inspires her sensitive portrayals of children, rather than physical beauty. And she particularly notes the mouth, which she considers the feature that most defines the character.

Alexander, one of Wippler's 1994 vinyl dolls from Sigikid, depicts a circa-1930s Berlin street urchin. The 27½-inch-high doll wears an outfit typical of that period: three-quarter-length pants with suspenders over long underpants, a white shirt, checked scarf, knee-length stockings, and laced boots. A peaked balloon cap tops *Alexander's* human-hair wig. He has painted eyes and is jointed at the head, arms, and legs.

Ilse Wippler, *Alexander*

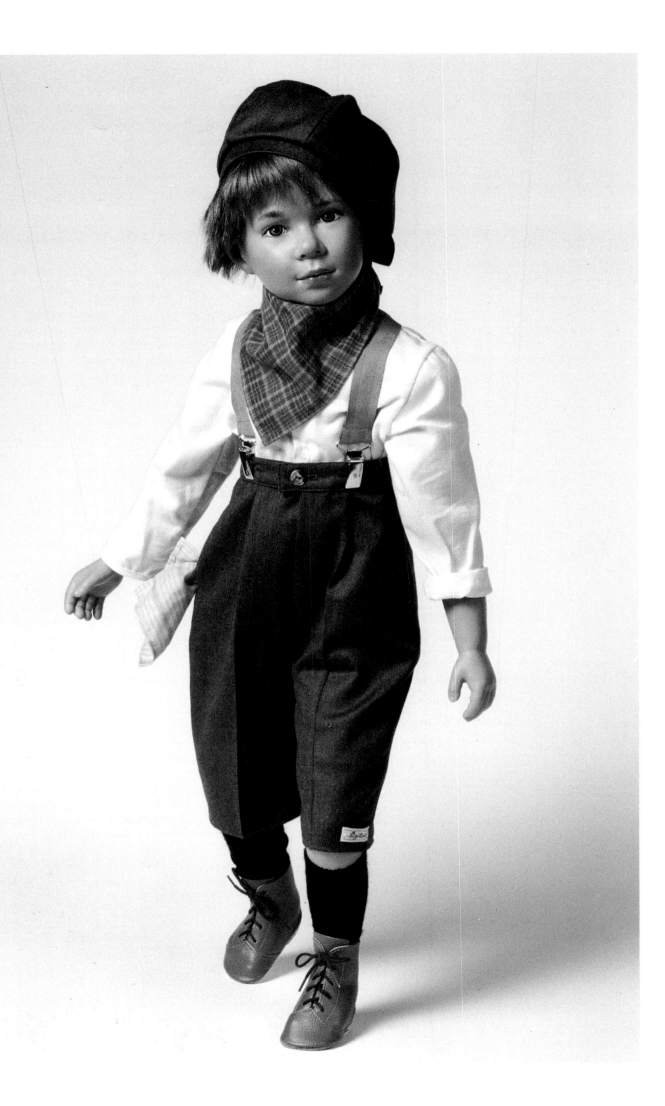

"*I* want my dolls to evoke an emotion that the viewer can relate to and feel good about: love, trust, innocence, joy, honor, or serenity," says the Los Angeles-born artist, now living in New York. Creating dolls for almost two decades, sixty-seven-year-old Singer is quite prolific, making more than fifty dolls a year. As she's designed dolls for the direct-marketing firms The Ashton-Drake Galleries and Danbury Mint, examples of her work are found in many collections.

Twenty-seven-inch-high *Christiane* is not a typical work for the artist, as the girl is larger and a bit older-looking than the toddlers and children for which Singer is known. "The older I get, the more grandchildren I get," explains Singer, "and I realize that I just have a real heart for children." *Christiane* is porcelain on a cloth body with a wire armature; its porcelain parts are jointed at the head, wrists, and ankles. Made in 1993, she was among the artist's best-selling pieces. Singer began working in porcelain in 1978 after getting a glimpse of some porcelain dolls at the first doll club meeting she attended. (Prior to that she'd been making apple-head dolls, and was even nicknamed the Apple Doll Queen!) Having worked for two ceramics firms making porcelain flowers and designing statues and figurines, Singer says it was only natural that she start sculpting dolls. "I immensely enjoy creating with my hands, and I've acquired many skills over the years that are helpful in dollmaking," she explains. "It seemed very natural and comfortable to pursue creations in this field."

Jeanne C. Singer, *Christiane*

"I like children, and I like dolls; that's why I began making dolls," says this artist, who sculpted her first doll in 1983. Growing up in postwar Germany, Stein only owned one doll, upon which she lavished all her attention *and* a large wardrobe she made herself. She was trained to be a commercial artist but took up dollmaking after taking a pottery course.

Stein's earliest works were sculpted of clay. Although she still sculpts her originals of clay, she makes molds of her sculptures and casts them in porcelain, the medium of the 1992 *Boy with His Teddy*. This doll, crafted in her Langenau-Albeck studio, has a mohair wig hand-knotted by a local hairdresser and hand-painted gray eyes. His cloth body contains a wire armature so that he can be posed. His clothing, like that of all Stein's dolls, is crafted of all natural materials, right down to his leather oxfords.

Most of the artist's dolls are crafted in limited editions of ten to twenty-five pieces, and she also does some one-of-a-kinds. However, the German doll manufacturer Sigikid produces vinyl versions of her dolls in editions of 500.

Typically, Stein's dolls depict young children because, she explains, "I have always loved to study the faces of very young children. There is so much pantomime and body language to clue you in to their private worlds, their sensitivity. Older children and adults learn to mask their emotions; their true feelings are often hard to discern." She adds, "I like to make boys more than girls, but most collectors seem to prefer girls, and I have to follow the trend."

Wiltrud Stein, *Boy with His Teddy*

*T*his one-of-a-kind creation by New Jersey artist Nancy Wiley features a twenty-six-inch-high doll and two marionettes. The name for the piece comes from the maiden puppet's elaborate overdress with its fitted waist and a draped cutaway overskirt, which is called a polonaise. The large doll has a porcelain head, arms, and legs on a cloth body; a human-hair wig that the artist has painted white; and painted blue eyes. Its body, arms, and legs are wired so that the doll can be posed. The marionettes are all-porcelain.

"I am interested in promoting the doll to be a respected and accepted art form," says Wiley, who describes her dolls as "three-dimension paintings." If you look at this vignette, you'll see what she means. The doll's baroque-style costume features a brocade dress with the skirt pulled back to reveal a canvas panel. The artist has painted a scene on this panel to provide a backdrop for the marionettes, which are held in front of it. The panels of the doll's skirt form curtains around the scenery backdrop, completing what is, in essence, a miniature stage set.

Wiley has been creating original, one-of-a-kind dolls since 1987. While the quality, beauty, and exceptional detailing of *Polonaise* is typical of her work, she notes that she creates dolls representing "all kinds of people and all kinds of expressions. Each doll is totally different to me." Still, she leaves the interpretation of her work to the individual viewer.

Nancy Wiley, *Polonaise*

*T*exas artist Pamela Phillips is a relative newcomer to the doll world, but is quickly establishing a reputation for her porcelain children. Phillips began drawing and painting portraits as a child. She majored in fine arts at Abilene Christian University, Abilene, Texas, and worked as a portraitist until 1990. "That year," Phillips says, "I saw a little girl who was just so outstanding looking that I wanted to do more than a portrait of her, so decided to use her as the model for a porcelain doll." Unfortunately, Phillips was unable to find anyone to help her overcome the many difficulties involved with porcelain dollmaking, so struggled for two years before completing two dolls that satisfied her personal standards. She showed them to Thomas Boland of Chicago, who represents some of America's top artists. Boland was impressed with her dolls and displayed them at his booth at the 1993 American International Toy Fair, a large trade event.

Because of the positive response to her work at the Toy Fair, Phillips is now concentrating on porcelain dollmaking and creates both one-of-a-kinds and limited editions of twenty to twenty-five pieces. All her dolls are portraits of actual children. What appeals to her, and shines through her work, is the simplicity and freshness of youth. "We all start out with no cares, no worry or stress lines in our faces," Phillips says. "It is this serenity that I try to capture in my dolls." *Nizhonii*, a prototype for the New York City-based doll company, Seymour Mann, Inc., is typical of her work. The twenty-five-inch-high doll has a porcelain head, arms, and legs on a cloth body, and is jointed at the neck, shoulders, elbows, and hips.

Pamela Phillips, *Nizhonii*

*M*ary and *Emily* are eighteen and nineteen inches tall and are limited to editions of 200 each. They wear hand-embroidered blouses, hand-knitted cardigans, and smocked lawn skirts. The three dolls in the toy shop vignette are named *Violet, Henrietta,* and *Sam.* They are twenty-one inches high and limited to editions of seventy-five each. All five of these dolls have porcelain heads and hands; their bodies, arms, and legs are wood. They have human-hair wigs and inset glass eyes.

The Roches have been creating original dolls since 1982. Prior to that they spent several years making reproductions of antique dolls. Today this husband-and-wife team is well known for gentle portrayals of children, which they describe as "strong and unsentimental images." The dolls are not portraits of actual children, but rather, explain the artists, "they are our own vision." The couple's dolls are noted for their pensive expressions, their charming contemporary costumes (they are created with natural fabrics and many of them feature hand-knitted sweaters and jackets), and their multiple-jointed, hand-carved wooden bodies. Joints at the neck, shoulders, elbows, wrists, hips, and knees enable the Roches' dolls to be positioned in a wide variety of lifelike poses. Michael does all the carving of the bodies and limbs; Lynne does all the painting.

Lynne and Michael Roche, *Sisters, Mary* and *Emily*

Overleaf. Lynne and Michael Roche, *Violet,*
Henrietta, and *Sam*

*B*orn in Michigan but currently residing in Georgia, Antonette Cely made her first original doll in 1983. So spectacular was her work that just a few years later, in the spring of 1986, she was invited to join the prestigious National Institute of American Doll Artists. Cely began her professional career as a theatrical costumer, and her expert skills as a seamstress and vast knowledge of the history of fashion are reflected in her dolls, many of which wear elegant period costumes. A good example of this is *Lucille's* 1940s-style gown, made of cotton net trimmed with embroidered flowers. Under the gown is a mauve silk slip, and on the doll's feet are lavender suede shoes.

Several events spurred Cely's interest in dollmaking. The first was a visit to the home of costume designer William Ivy Long. During the visit Long was busily embroidering a cloth doll of Marie Antoinette, which Cely found fascinating. Later, she stayed at the home of a doll collector who introduced her to a wider world of dolls. Then she found a book on Japanese dollmaking that inspired her to create a cloth doll based on the Oriental designs.

Though the style of Cely's dolls has changed over the years, she still uses fabric, although you may find that difficult to believe when looking at *Lucille*. Her head is constructed of Swiss cotton broadcloth over Sculpey III; the body and limbs are broadcloth. The doll is an unjointed, fifteen-inch-high, one-of-a-kind creation. Made in 1989, it has an acrylic fleece wig and inset eyes made of Sculpey/Fimo and painted blue.

Antonette Cely, *Lucille*

FayZah Spanos was born on the Greek island of Kalymnos, but has lived in the United States since she was eleven years old. In 1985, after marriage and the birth of her first child, Spanos began buying and repairing old dolls that she then sold to supplement her family's income. This work led to an interest in ceramics, and soon she was taking classes in making reproduction dolls. By 1986 she had sculpted her first original doll, a portrait of her son Theodore. The following year, the artist had completed her first two limited-edition porcelain dolls. Today Spanos has her own company, Precious Heirloom Dolls, Inc., of Tarpon Springs, Florida, through which her porcelain and vinyl dolls are sold. Edition sizes range from just twenty pieces to as many as 2,500. Spanos also designs dolls for the Danbury Mint.

"I want collectors of my dolls to feel the love, warmth, and joy that children bring into our lives," says Spanos, who is known for her enchanting porcelain and vinyl toddlers and infants. *Jacques*, a portrait of the artist's nephew, is typical of her work. The original was sculpted in Plastilene clay and reproduced in both porcelain and vinyl. The porcelain edition is twenty-two inches high; the vinyl is twenty-six inches. The dolls in both editions have cloth bodies, are jointed at the shoulders and hips, and wear perky navy-blue sailor suits and hats with gold trim.

FayZah Spanos, *Jacques*

The artist doll movement is still in its infancy in Australia, where Karen Blandford creates her soulful portrayals of children and young women. But the artist is used to breaking new ground; while in her teens she became the first woman to be apprenticed by Australia's State Rail Authority, and during her first year on the job was named Railways Apprentice of the Year. Although creating original dolls is a far cry from painting railroad cars and signs, Blandford's determination to do the very best she can in anything she undertakes has, once again, brought her recognition, this time as one of her country's leading doll artists.

Blandford began making reproduction dolls in the mid-1980s and created her first original in 1989. "I'd seen dolls in shops," she says, "but they were too expensive, so I decided to make my own." Moving from reproductions to originals seemed a natural progression for her, but she didn't jump into it without preparation. Before creating her own dolls she attended a sculpting seminar that was offered in the United States by German sculptor Theo Menzenbach. Although she denigrates the first original she made, the beauty of the three dolls in *Summer Afternoon*, completed in 1992 and 1993, shows how quickly she mastered this art form. Ranging from fifteen to thirty-five inches in height, these dolls have porcelain heads, arms, and legs on cloth bodies with wire armatures. They have handmade mohair wigs, inset paperweight eyes, and are costumed in voile and French lace.

Karen Blandford, *Summer Afternoon*

"Art was never a conscious goal, it was just always a part of my life," says artist Elke Hutchens. Born in Berlin shortly after the end of World War II, she studied art at the Hamburg Art Institute before moving to England, and later to Alaska. It was while living in Alaska that she took up sculpting as a way to express herself. "I learned to express my feelings in my work, my feelings of homesickness and the anxiety of finding myself in unfamiliar surroundings, mixed with the exhilaration of new and different experiences," she says.

It wasn't until years later, after she married, had children, and was living in Oregon, that she "embarked on the long and often frustrating process of creating my own original dolls." It was particularly frustrating for Hutchens because she took up this craft before it became popular, and there was very little information available. Doll shows at that time were limited mostly to antique dolls and reproductions of antiques, so Hutchens started selling her work at gift shows. This proved highly successful for her. Today her company, Elke's Originals of Beaverton, Oregon, employs more than thirty people and produces thousands of dolls a year.

The dolls shown here and on the following pages were made from 1989 to 1991 and are very illustrative of Hutchens' work. They all have porcelain heads and limbs on cloth bodies and German hand-blown glass eyes. They range in height from nineteen to twenty-four inches and in edition size from 250 to 500 pieces.

Elke Hutchens, *Annabelle*, *Alicia*, *Aurora*, and *Aubra*

Overleaf right. Elke Hutchens, *Victoria*

Overleaf left. Elke Hutchens, *Braelyn*

*T*his porcelain creation is typical of the beautiful, ethereal creations of Eveline Frings. In order to "stir the imagination, to invite you to dream, to reflect, to find some aspect of yourself at the moment of viewing," Frings says she tries to create a dreamy atmosphere with her work. Her dolls, undeniably beautiful, are not made for sale. "Each piece," Frings feels, "is an act of love to be shared with others through exhibitions, photographs, and books."

This blond sister has all the hallmarks of a Frings doll: slender, elongated arms and legs; straight nose; large, wide-set eyes; and long hair. She is dressed in the finest antique laces and adorned with tiny silk flowers and pearls. Her eyes are blown glass; her mohair wig was dyed and styled by Frings.

The Austrian-born artist has lived all over the world: in the United States, Belgium, France, and Germany, where she currently resides when she's not working as a flight attendant. One of those people who was always drawing or painting, Frings crafted her first doll in 1986 "to create a source of inspiration for my daughter." Today she works in a variety of media and says that her enjoyment in dollmaking comes from the combination of art forms—painting, carving, sculpting, and costuming—that goes into each creation.

Eveline Frings, *One of Three Sisters*

*R*egina Sandreuter is a native of Munich. Abhinavo Sandreuter was born in Basel, Switzerland. The two artists met in India and after returning to Europe together decided to pursue a joint artistic venture. They settled on dollmaking and created their first originals in 1981. The Sandreuters' early dolls were called Regina's Traumfiguren (Regina's Dream Figures) and had an otherworldliness about them. They were feminine creations clad in Indian cottons; some had sculpted hair, others had hair of metallic yarns or feathers. When these dolls were exhibited in 1982 they were heralded for their beauty and dreamlike quality, and the Sandreuters were accepted into the European community of modern doll artists.

Regina's Traumfiguren quickly sold, but not to children or doll collectors. Most were purchased by international jewelers and used for window displays. This was not the purpose for which the Sandreuters had made them, so they decided to change direction and create more realistic-looking children. Many of their dolls are crafted in wood. However, *Victoria*, one of their 1994 creations, is all-porcelain. This 16½-inch-high doll has a mohair wig and green painted eyes, and is jointed at the neck, shoulders, elbows, wrists, waist, hips, and knees. *Victoria* is limited to an edition of one hundred pieces; however, the costume seen here appears on only thirty-five of the dolls. It features a printed cotton dress and cotton coat that is lined in silk and trimmed with velvet.

Regina & Abhinavo Sandreuter, *Victoria*

*A*lthough Regina and Abhinavo Sandreuter create beautiful porcelain dolls, they are best known for their wooden portrayals of contemporary children, such as *Marco with His Scooter*. A comparison of the lifelike face and form of this child to early woodens shows how far today's carvers have taken the artistry of dollmaking. In addition to the natural beauty of *Marco* and the Sandreuters' other wooden creations, all their dolls can be posed in many ways. Each doll has twelve joints, the Sandreuters point out, which offers a high level of flexibility. Many also come with active accessories, like Marco's scooter, which was specially designed for the doll.

The Sandreuters, who have their own company, Regina Sandreuter Charakterpuppen of Munich, sculpt the prototypes for their wood dolls in clay. Rough models are then mechanically reproduced in maple, after which the Sandreuters carve the facial features and sand, paint, and varnish the dolls. "We prefer to keep facial expressions nonspecific and calm to allow for a variety of emotional responses," note the Sandreuters. "We'd rather have the viewer's emotion mirrored."

Created in 1992, 17½-inch-high *Marco with His Scooter* is limited to an edition of 240; his costume is limited to an edition of fifty. Like all the Sandreuters' dolls, *Marco* has a mohair wig, made to the artists' specifications, and wears clothing using only natural fibers.

Regina & Abhinavo Sandreuter, *Marco with His Scooter*

*S*andra Babin has been creating one-of-a-kind dolls since 1985. Her works are sculpted from natural stone clay. Born and raised in Louisiana, the artist loved dolls as a child and began collecting antique dolls as an adult. She then tried her hand at making reproductions of antiques and, after a few successful efforts, turned to creating her own originals. Today she is best known for her portrayals of pensive children and young girls, such as the two girls in *Colors United*. The taller of these dolls is twenty-nine inches; the other is twenty-six. Their heads, arms, and legs are in wax over natural stone clay; their bodies are constructed of stretch lace over fiberfill, foil, and wire-wrapped armatures. The dolls are jointed at the shoulders. Both have synthetic-hair wigs and inset European glass eyes and wear dresses made from an antique eyelet petticoat.

In discussing her depictions of children, the self-taught artist says, "I don't have a concept in mind when I begin to sculpt; my dolls evolve as I work. However, I try to create a look of innocence and antiquity." This look is enhanced by the antique fabrics and trims she often uses for her dolls' costumes. Children are Babin's favorite subject, but by no means her only one. She has also created adult figures and angels, plus a few Father Christmases. In addition to her one-of-a-kinds, on which she does all the work herself, Babin has designed dolls for the Franklin Mint of Franklin Center, Pennsylvania.

Sandra F. Babin, *Colors United*

A 1994 doll from the Donauwörth studios of Käthe Kruse Puppen GmbH, *Paquita* is made using basically the same production methods that have been used by this company since Kruse founded it in 1910. Most of the work is done by hand, with each doll taking an average of twelve hours to complete. (The factory employs about sixty-five people, and there are an additional seventy-five part-time employees who work from their homes.) Part of the Faithful Child series, twenty-one-inch *Paquita* has a composition head on a nettle cloth body stuffed with reindeer hair. Underneath her red wool camel-hair coat, she wears a white-and-blue checked dress; she's limited to an edition of thirty pieces.

This doll, and all the dolls being created by the Käthe Kruse firm today, are crafted under the guidance of Andrea-Kathrin and Stephen Christenson who, along with the family of Prince Albrecht zu Castell-Castell, bought the workshops from the Kruse family in 1990. Andrea played with Kruse dolls when she was growing up, and in her current position has tried to uphold the company's traditional style of elegant simplicity that she was so attracted to as a child. She says she wants the Kruse dolls to remain "cozy and warm, like little infants that just ask for hugging and loving." Although the Kruse dolls are made to be "a child for a child," in the words of the company's founder, even the new ones hold a great appeal for collectors today.

Käthe Kruse, *Paquita*

"*P*robably the most obvious feature of my work is its variety," says Swiss artist Elisabeth Flueler-Tomamichel, who has been making original dolls since 1977 and has also designed dolls for the Hamilton Collection. "I do not like to be fixed to a certain type of doll, nor to a size or a specific material," she says. Flueler-Tomamichel makes porcelain babies and children in editions of twenty to thirty pieces, as well as fantasy figures and dolls depicting musicians, dancers, or specific themes, such as *Ice*, the twenty-three-inch porcelain doll shown here. "With my first dolls, I just wanted to create something beautiful, but over the years I have tried to bring a statement into some special dolls too. I wanted them to be acting or to be in the middle of a movement," she says.

Ice, completed in 1989, is a stunning example of a figure captured in "the middle of a movement." The fluidity of this piece is enhanced by its costume. Over the doll's light-green underwear is a dress constructed of three layers of shiny, half-transparent fabric. Crystal icicles dangle from the gown's long points, and small icicles are also sewn onto the upper portion of the dress and the cap. A real crystal from the Swiss Alps is held in the doll's hand. About this piece the artist says, "I wanted to explain that we can feel cold, sometimes with the person nearest to us, but I believe we all have the power to extend a friendly hand, and the ice will melt if we just make the move."

Elisabeth Flueler-Tomamichel, *Ice*

*E*lisabeth Flueler-Tomamichel says, "I am obsessed with making dolls and spend all my time at it, but still only finish about ten to fifteen pieces a year." The artist works mainly in Super Sculpey and porcelain. With her limited-edition porcelain pieces, she says, "I change the head of each doll to adapt the features to the face I want to represent. I also change the costume for each doll." Thus all the dolls in any single edition are different. "I do not call these dolls one-of-a-kinds," she explains, "because I use the same mold several times." This partly accounts for the small number of dolls she creates annually. However, she also notes, "if there are two ways of making something, I choose the more difficult one, like making hands of porcelain that really hold an instrument. My gift is to make lovely hands and feet."

Prior to creating dolls, Flueler-Tomamichel worked as a fashion designer and pattern maker. Her expertise in this field and her skill as a sculptor are obvious in *Violin Player*. This twenty-six-inch doll has a porcelain head and hands (each hand was made in five pieces) on a cloth body with a wire armature. The period costume consists of silk stockings and knickers, a lace shirt and underpants, a waistcoat of antique Japanese brocade trimmed with antique buttons, a leather belt with a silver buckle and two hanging decorations, and a silk-satin coat lined with organza. The artist also made the doll's violin and bow.

Elisabeth Flueler-Tomamichel, *Violin Player*

While dollmaking has flourished in the United States, that is not the case with its neighbor to the north. That doesn't mean, however, that there is no exciting work being done by Canadian doll artists. Indeed, some of them are beginning to gain international recognition. Perhaps the best known is Madeleine Neill-St. Clair, whose *Sophie* is shown here.

"I have loved dolls since I was a child," says Neill-St. Clair, "and I have collected them as an adult." However, just collecting wasn't enough, and she began creating costumes for dolls. Next she got interested in making porcelain reproductions, and in 1978 she sculpted her first original doll. "I sculpt in water-based clays and finish the dolls in porcelain," says the artist, who has established Madeleine Neill-St. Clair Originals, Ltd., of Nanoose Bay, British Columbia. She creates one-of-a-kinds and limited-edition porcelain dolls; edition sizes range from twenty-five to fifty pieces. Neill-St. Clair has also designed for Paradise Galleries of La Jolla, California, and the Dynamic Group/Home Shopping Network.

Sophie, a 1994 creation, is twenty-six inches high and has a porcelain head, arms, and legs on a cotton body. The doll has a swivel neck and a wire armature inside the arms and legs to facilitate posing. Her outfit consists of a purple velvet jacket trimmed with colorful bands of fabric, ribbon, and embroidery; a white lace-trimmed cotton blouse; and a black cotton skirt with trim that matches the jacket's. In her hair is a garland of flowers.

Madeleine Neill-St. Clair, *Sophie*

*M*adeleine Neill-St. Clair is known for her sweet-faced porcelain babies and children up to age ten, such as *Mischief*. This 1994 creation is twenty-six inches high and, like all the artist's porcelain children, has a swivel head with a human-hair wig and inset glass eyes. Limited to an edition of thirty pieces, *Mischief* is a contemporary little girl dressed in a hand-knit yellow sweater, cotton print shorts with a matching hat, yellow socks, and red sneakers.

"I want my dolls to look bright, intelligent, charming," says the artist, "and I would like people to feel drawn to them in the same way that they are drawn to real children with attractive personalities. I try to have all my dolls 'tell a story,' either through their body positions, accessories, the way they relate to each other, or all three. I use," she adds, "only what I consider the very best of materials, fabrics, eyes, and wigs, most of which I make myself. I believe that you can't make anything good without good ingredients."

For the past several years Neill-St. Clair has been working with her eldest son, Gideon Hay. (Many of Hay's pieces depict animals in human clothing and poses, and present a whimsical look at human foibles.) "Since he and I have been working together my work has changed and developed in a lot of interesting directions due to our collaborations, as has his," she notes, adding, "I love my work and cannot imagine doing anything else."

Madeleine Neill-St. Clair, *Mischief*

"I have always loved dolls and began making reproduction dolls as a hobby and creative outlet for my sewing interests," says Peggy Dey. "This quickly led to an interest in sculpting my own creations." Best known for her joyous images of young girls, Dey created her first original doll in 1989; she now makes both one-of-a-kinds and limited-edition porcelain dolls, sold through her own company, Timeless Treasures of Lawrence, Kansas. Her edition sizes range from ten to fifty pieces. She has also designed dolls for Effanbee Doll Company of Linden, New Jersey, and the Danbury Mint.

"I complete all of the work on my Timeless Treasures dolls," says Dey, "including cleaning the greenware, painting, and designing and making the costumes. My son assists with pouring the porcelain slip and assembly." Because the artist has no other staff, her production is limited. All of her dolls are fully jointed with plastic armatures. "Their costumes," Dey explains, "are designed specifically to fit the personality of each doll."

Paige is typical of Dey's work. Twenty-eight inches high, the doll has a porcelain head, arms, and legs on a cloth body. The wig is of synthetic mohair; the inset eyes are green glass paperweights. The doll wears a striped pinafore over a black-print dress trimmed with cotton lace and a floppy hat embellished with flowers. She carries a white wicker basket filled with flowers.

Peggy Dey, *Paige*

This German native is known to collectors for the high-priced vinyl versions of her work that have been manufactured by the German toy company Sigikid in the past and by Gotz, another German firm, in recent years. It was a landmark event in the doll-collecting world when her first vinyl dolls were released in 1989, as up until this point vinyl was not highly valued as a medium for quality artist dolls. Those early vinyls, as well as the ones made today, are manufactured versions of the very limited-edition porcelain originals the artist makes in her own studio, like thirty-six-inch *Lilly* created by Esche in 1989.

Always interested in the arts, Esche worked in an art gallery and painted in her spare time until the birth of her daughter in 1968. As a Christmas present to her husband, the artist sculpted a clay head of their child. This started her on a line of cloth dolls and puppets, which she sold to shops until 1978. That was the year she modeled, in wax, portraits of her grandparents as children after finding an old photo of them. "I was taken by the children's serious expressions, expressions children today do not normally have in photos," recalls Esche. "Today we photograph children smiling or laughing." Even today, sixteen years later, the dolls created by this artist retain the solemn innocence of the children in that photo.

Sabine Esche, *Lilly*

When Sabine Esche began working in porcelain, she stopped making portrait dolls of her family and started crafting interpretive works based on children she saw around her. "I would see children when I was traveling," Esche says, "who appealed to me in some way, not necessarily because they were beautiful, but because they had something in their faces: expressive eyes or a certain mouth. I would take photos of them and then work from those photos; but of course, the artistic part of the work enters in." She compares her dolls to a still life painting: "If it is a painting of flowers, the painter is painting the flowers as she sees them. She is interpreting them realistically, *but as she sees them.*"

Before she begins sculpting, Esche will sometimes make some sketches, particularly if she feels the children in the photos she's working from don't show enough expression. Her original sculptures are done in clay and take at least ten days to complete. From the clay model she makes a plaster cast, which she uses to pour the porcelain head and limbs (most of her dolls have leather bodies). This is when the artist gets to work on her favorite part of the dollmaking process: painting the face and setting the eyes. She enjoys this because it is at this point that the doll comes to life. "I want to conserve something young and beautiful that does not age," says the artist. "I want my dolls to be a victory over time." Her one-of-a-kind *Felice* was made in 1993 and stands thirty-six inches high.

Sabine Esche, *Felice*

*M*aryanne Oldenburg began creating original dolls in 1973 because, she says, "the dollhouses I was building needed 'families.'" She founded Oldenburg Originals of Waldo, Wisconsin, and designs dolls for Georgetown Collection. The artist is best known for her porcelain babies, toddlers, and children, many of which are based on actual children she has either photographed herself or found pictures of in magazines and newspapers. She creates one-of-a-kinds and limited-edition porcelain dolls from her original Plasticene sculptures; edition sizes usually range from fifteen to thirty pieces.

Jessica is typical of the artist's work, which captures the essence of childhood, its sweetness and innocence. This sixteen-inch-high doll has a porcelain head, arms, and legs on a cloth body with an armature that allows the doll to be posed. *Jessica* has painted green eyes and a kanekalon wig. Her outfit consists of a white linen dress trimmed with lace, a lace underskirt, and lace-trimmed underwear. A garland of silk roses adorns her head, and she holds a bouquet of similar roses in her hands. "Each of my dolls has a handmade accessory," the artist notes, "because I want my dolls to be animated, to be posed doing something."

Maryanne Oldenburg, *Jessica*

After losing his job in a small-town hardware store R. John Wright turned to dollmaking. He had a friend who made porcelain dolls and thought maybe he could make a living doing something similar. He eschewed porcelain, however, choosing to work with felt as he was an admirer of the creations made by Steiff, a German firm famous for its early felt dolls and animals. Wright made his first original doll in 1976 and has since gone on to found his own company, R. John Wright Dolls, Inc., located in Cambridge, New York. The artist is still involved in every step of production.

Wright's early dolls had seamed faces, similar to Steiff's creations. Then the artist discovered the Lenci dolls, which have seamless molded-felt faces. Preferring the Lenci look, he developed his own production methods for creating molded heads. He quickly gained recognition for his exquisitely crafted felt dolls, many of which depict characters from children's stories and nursery rhymes such as Snow White and the Seven Dwarfs, Pinocchio, and Jack and Jill. However, the artist also creates charming portrait dolls like *Arthur*, which is a seventeen-inch-high doll of his eldest son, Arthur Wright. The doll has a mohair wig and brown painted eyes; it is jointed at the neck, hips, and shoulders. *Arthur* wears an authentic child's sailor suit and hat, which are removable, and holds a fully rigged wood-and-metal sailboat. Created in a limited edition of 500, *Arthur* is from the artist's Little Brother/Little Sister series.

R. John Wright, *Arthur*

*B*orn in Stuttgart, Germany, Renate Höckh began painting thirty years ago and has not stopped since in her quest for beauty. A self-taught artist, she took up sculpting in 1980 because, she explains, "I find working in three dimensions easier than two." She adds that she sees "no division between dolls and sculptures and therefore I prefer to call my works 'figurines.'"

Each of the three figures in *Balinese Siblings* depicted here is a one-of-a-kind sculpted in clay and cast in porcelain, which is how all of Höckh's dolls are made. (The elder sister is thirty-one inches high.) These dolls, however, were also created in a special vinyl edition by Dollmakers Originals International of Glenmoore, Pennsylvania, in 1993, and a portion of the proceeds from their sale went to UNICEF. Höckh has been working with Dollmakers Originals since 1992; they manufacture vinyl and porcelain editions of some of her one-of-a-kind sculptures.

Höckh, who now lives in the Alsace-Lorraine region of France, has earned a reputation for creating daring and unconventional pieces, rather than sweet little dolls. She gets her inspiration from "deep inside" and does not sculpt from photographs or models. The artist says, "Everyone is special, and I want to show this. I get very excited each time a new idea of portraying someone takes shape. This, to me, feels like an act of creation."

Renate Höckh, *Balinese Siblings*

*S*tephanie Blythe and Susan Snodgrass began collaborating on making dolls and miniature room boxes in 1977. Now the artists are best known for their fairies, which they introduced in 1981. But they also create other fantasy figures, such as goddesses and mermaids. Most pieces are one-of-a-kinds, although they'll do an occasional doll in a limited edition of twenty pieces. Their work has been exhibited at the Musée des Arts Décoratif at the Louvre, the American Craft Museum in New York City, the Toy Museum of Atlanta, and the Miniature Museum of Kansas City.

Blythe, a graduate of the Philadelphia College of Art, worked as an illustrator, art instructor, and textile designer before turning to dollmaking. It is she who sculpts and paints the original porcelain dolls. Snodgrass creates the lavish costumes for the pieces using antique laces, metallic fabrics, silk flower petals, and, sometimes, real butterfly wings. She studied at the Art Institute of Chicago and the Goodman Theater and has designed clothing, costumes, and jewelry for fashion companies and mixed-media exhibits.

Shoe Fairy is typical of these artists' fantasy dolls, many of which inhabit antique objects such as old shoes, teacups, or champagne glasses, or stand on crystal foundations. This eight-inch, all-porcelain fairy is a one-of-a-kind. The fairy's eyes are sculpted closed. The doll's wig is constructed of dyed Tibetan lamb's wool, the wings are made of hand-painted silk, and the costume is a combination of antique fabrics and lace. The doll is posed in one of a pair of antique shoes decorated with lace, opals, and Austrian crystals.

Stephanie Blythe and Susan Snodgrass, *Shoe Fairy*

*L*inda Mason is one of America's most loved doll artists. She is known not only for her poignant portrayals of the innocence and beauty of childhood, but also for her personal vivaciousness and generosity. The artist began making reproduction dolls in 1977, she says, "as a way to combine my love of art, my love of dolls, and my love of children." By 1978 she had sculpted her first original doll. She now has her own company, Linda Mason Originals of Benicia, California, and also designs dolls for the Georgetown Collection.

Mason sculpts her dolls in clay. These sculptures are then used to create molds for her porcelain and vinyl dolls, which are issued in limited editions. The artist also occasionally creates one-of-a-kinds. For her limited-edition pieces, Mason assigns some aspects of the dollmaking process to others; however, she personally does all the work on her porcelain dolls' heads (including pouring, firing, cleaning, painting, setting eyes, and hairstyling) and all the painting of her vinyls.

Laurel is typical of the artist's beautifully detailed work. This twenty-inch-high doll has a porcelain head, arms, and legs, and a cloth body with a wire armature. Her wig is made of human hair, and she has brown glass inset eyes. Made in 1989 and limited to an edition of 150 pieces, *Laurel* wears a gingham print dress and pinafore.

Linda Mason, *Laurel*

*A*nnette Himstedt is one of the world's best-known doll artists. She made her first doll, crafted of stone and cloth, in 1975 and began working in porcelain four years later. In December 1982 the first public exhibition of her dolls was staged at Ludwig Beck's, a Munich store that was a pioneer in exhibiting artist dolls in Germany. No venue could have been more appropriate, for Himstedt has always been a leader in the doll-artist movement herself. Her early dolls were one-of-a-kinds; then in 1986 she opened her own workshop in Spain to produce her dolls in vinyl. (Her vinyl creations are distributed in the United States by Mattel; the artist distributes them in Europe.) Today there is such demand for her dolls that even her porcelains are issued in editions ranging in size from twenty-five to ninety pieces.

As a child the German artist painted portraits. "Later," she says, "I changed from painting to modeling. When I started working with porcelain, I wanted to make 'children out of porcelain,' not real dolls. Today's children seem so lively, open, and natural to me, they are like no other generation. I love to capture them in porcelain." *Mohan* and *Mohini* are typical of her work; they are large, contemporary children with porcelain heads, shoulder plates, arms, and legs, and cloth bodies. *Mohan* is twenty-nine inches high and is costumed in a hand-dyed silk blouse and trousers. Twenty-eight-inch *Mohini* wears an Indian chiffon blouse lined with French silk and decorated with hand-embroidered flowers, sequins, and beads. Her trousers are of Indian silk embroidered with beads; her veil is of chiffon with hand-embroidered flowers and antique glass beads. Both are limited to editions of eighty pieces.

Annette Himstedt, *Mohan* and *Mohini*

*T*n 1984 after the death of her young daughter, Dawn, Marilyn Bolden began sculpting dolls. "I knew I had to do something with my life for the sake of my husband and son," she says, "so I turned to my artwork as a refuge. Making dolls became the best outlet for me to deal with this tragedy." Today, Bolden's days are filled with dollmaking as she and her husband and son work on the production of Mari-Dawn Dolls, based in Clearwater, Florida.

When the artist began creating dolls, she did mostly commissions for one-of-a-kind portrait dolls. She still creates some portraits, such as *Molly*, a portrayal of Bolden's niece. Made of porcelain, this twenty-seven-inch blonde-haired beauty, created in 1992, looks out of hazel blown-glass eyes. Her dress of iridescent teal taffeta is accented by a white collar.

Most of Bolden's dolls, like *Molly*, are limited to editions of around 100 pieces. She also creates some smaller editions of under ten pieces, as well as continuing to do her one-of-a-kinds, which are made of Super Sculpey. In 1992 Bolden began working with the Hamilton Collection in Jacksonville, Florida, which produces her designs in much larger editions. The artist's best known work to date is her *Millie Claire*, a twenty-two-inch fashion doll especially created to showcase the Philip Douglas Cosmetic Corporation's beauty line.

Bolden enjoys creating young girls and feels that the best part of her dolls is their sculpting, particularly that of the nose and mouth. "I feel that each doll I make is a part of me," she says. "When people buy my dolls, they are not just buying a product. I love every one that I do."

Marilyn Bolden, *Molly*

"*My* love of art and the need to be creative, as well as a life-long love of dolls, evolved into my desire to make porcelain dolls," says this California-born artist, who sculpted her first original doll in 1992. *The Enchantress* was created in 1993. Thirty-six inches high, the porcelain doll has a human-hair wig and wears a medieval-style gold-embossed black velvet dress with a train. Crystals, stars, and other mystical trinkets complete the ensemble. Most of Thanos' works, like this one, have cloth bodies and are jointed at the neck, elbow, hips, and knees. This doll happens to be a one-of-a-kind, but many of the works the dollmaker creates under the name of Charleen Thanos Originals, her Portland, Oregon, company, are done in editions of 5 to 250 pieces.

The Enchantress is typical of the artist's works, which generally depict girls from the ages of five to eighteen. Her works have that classic doll look, and often wear period costumes. Thanos studied art in college and began making reproductions of antiques in the 1980s. "I wish my dolls to evoke a feeling of confidence, peace, calm, and delight," says Thanos of her originals. "I want people to look at my dolls and feel glad to be alive." A perfectionist, it is important to her that her dolls have smoothly cleaned porcelain, perfectly painted features, and fitted clothing. "I design my dolls from within my heart and would like the love I feel for this undertaking to shine through in each of my dolls."

Charleen Thanos, *The Enchantress*

*E*dna Dali began her professional career in 1972 as a social worker in Israel. She had to give up this job in 1977 when she and her family moved to England. There she enrolled in art and sculpting courses and began designing crafts using fine textiles and antique materials. Four years later she moved to the United States where she met several well-known American doll artists and became fascinated with the world of dollmaking. In 1981, after some additional courses in sculpting, she created her first original doll.

After returning to Israel with her husband and three children, the artist continued to make dolls, quickly gaining international recognition for her poignant portrayals of children. "Their dream-like look," says Dali, "hides the unknown. Their dreaming can be interpreted by the viewer as she or he prefers." Today she creates one-of-a-kind works, such as *Dolls in Hat Shop*, as well as wax-over-porcelain dolls in limited editions of 50 to 100 pieces.

Dolls in Hat Shop features two twenty-six-inch-high dolls. Both have Fimo heads, arms, and legs, and cloth bodies with wire armatures. They have mohair wigs and inset, German hand-blown crystal eyes. The redhead has green eyes and wears an antique green velvet gown trimmed with handmade antique silk flowers and lace. The brunette has dark blue eyes and wears an antique cream lace dress adorned with silk flowers. Completing this hat shop vignette are a variety of hats, an old Persian carpet, and a standing antique mirror.

Edna Dali, *Dolls in Hat Shop*

ACKNOWLEDGEMENTS

The authors wish to thank Dorothy S., Elizabeth A. and Evelyn J. Coleman for sharing so much of their knowledge about the history of dolls through their many books (including the two-volume *The Collector's Encyclopedia of Dolls*) and magazine articles; John Darcy Noble, curator emeritus of the Doll and Toy Collection of the Museum of the City of New York and contributing editor to *Dolls* magazine, for inspiring our interest in antique dolls and sharing his love of them through his delightful magazine articles; Diane Goff Yupatoff and Barry Leo Delaney for helping us with our research on Lenci; Robert Obojski for helping us compile photographs of antique dolls; Susanne Denk-Romney for generously lending us her Madame Alexander doll to photograph; Robert Campbell Rowe, president of Collector Communications Corporation and publisher of *Dolls*, for suggesting we do this book, and for his many efforts toward broadening interest in dolls as collectible works of art; and to the artists, photographers and auction houses who supplied photographs of dolls.

PHOTO CREDITS

Pages 9, 11, and 16: Courtesy of Sotheby's London; page 13: Courtesy of Richard W. Withington, Inc., Hillsboro, New Hampshire; pages 15 and 22: Courtesy of James and Shari McMasters of McMasters', Cambridge, Ohio; page 17: Courtesy of Barbara Frasher of Frasher's, Oak Grove, Missouri; page 20: Courtesy of Käthe Kruse Puppen GmbH; page 23: Lynton Gardiner (From the Collection of Anne Votaw); page 26: Lynton Gardiner (From the Personal Collection of Susanne Denk-Romney); page 83: Barbara and Larry Mordock; page 85: Larry Mordock; page 89: Nick Nicholson; page 101: David White; page 113: Bruce Rouse.